Stories About
MAMA

EMBRACING HER LEGACY,
HONORING HER LIFE

A Compilation By Bestselling Author

DR. KAREN MAXFIELD-LUNKIN

Stories About Mama

Unless otherwise notated, scripture quotations are taken from the Holy Bible, New Living Translation, copyright ©1996, 2004, 2015 by Tyndale House Foundation. Used by permission of Tyndale House Publishers, Carol Stream, Illinois 60188. All rights reserved.

ISBN 979-8-9855023-3-6

Printed and bound in the United States of America

Book Designed by Brand It Beautifully™
www.branditbeautifully.com
allison@imallisondenise.com

Table of Contents

HOW IT ALL BEGAN

Re-Building Kingdom One Story at a Time

"Your people will rebuild the ancient ruins
and will raise up the age-old foundations;
you will be called Repairer of broken walls,
Restorer of streets with dwellings."
— Isaiah 58:12 (KJV)

THE SYNCHRONICITY OF THIS MOMENT

Comfortably cornered in my favorite coffee shop, Congolese worship music, my writing muse richly filling my earbuds, my face wet with warm tears as the significance of *this moment* of writing, engulfed me. My fingers typed with no apprehension of anyone else seeing me in this emotional state. *I am here*, I thought, as a bridge between the past and present, pen readied with all of the seeds of possibilities for the future at the tip end of my pen. I'm praying as I type - petitioning Him - asking for a deeper understanding, wisdom, nuggets of knowing that only He can give. Understanding. The weight of telling our incomparable Black mothers' stories swelled heavy as the belly of a mother anticipating the soon birth.

I understand the assignment, to cooperate with the pains of birthing – push during the contractions, breathe, *breathe*, *BREATHE!* In, out, in, out, in, out. Breathe in the inspiration, new thoughts and insights conceived from the joining of history and desire for healing reconciliation; breathe out the words of light and healing onto the page.

With the crowning of the head, I'm filled with anticipation and infinite gratitude for what will emerge from what was; through me here, *in this present moment*, stretching out as a bridge to what will be! Knowing that this baby isn't mine, that she belongs to The Father, Our Father – I *whisper another prayer for direction* as I rest my eyes and breathe in deeply, looking down at my phone to this timely anointed text from Dr. Michelle McCormick, one of the co-authors:

> *"Praying for your continual strength as you continue*
> *through the process of this assignment. The weight is*
> *always the heaviest near the end of the assignment. I have*
> *your arms lifted in prayer!"*

Ironically, the historic U.S. Senate confirmation hearings were underway for Judge Ketanji Brown Jackson potential appointment to the Supreme Court. I watched in awe as she demonstrated so eloquently the beauty, brilliance, resilience, hope, humility, and glory of the Black woman about whom we are writing. As she fielded the questioning with elegance and grace, tears continued flowing as I embraced the unprecedented gravity and significance of writing THIS book in *this moment*. I could only smile in complete admiration as I have so many times at my Father. Once again, in *this moment*, appeared a visual representation of the words I carefully penned onto the page.

A LEGACY LIFTING HISTORICAL ACCOUNT

Stories About Mama is a compilation of narratives from ten authors whose mothers were born within a 30 year span (1924 – 1954), smack dab in the middle of the Jim Crow era (1896-1954) a time when many African Americans, women included, were sharecroppers. Interviewing my aunts between the ages of 85 and 94 (at the time of this writing), I learned how back-breaking the work was – not to mention the mental and emotional toll the era took on their psyche.

A VIEW FROM THE JIM CROW ERA AND SHARECROPPING (1866-1955)

"After the [Civil] war, the federal government was called upon by Northerners to confiscate the lands of plantation owners who fought against the North and redistribute it among ex-slaves. The government refused, leaving almost all of the freed Blacks desperately poor. In order to feed themselves and their families, many of them agreed to return to work the land of their former masters in return for a share of the crops they raised. The remaining shares would be used to pay rent and buy supplies. Unfortunately, what frequently resulted was peonage – the unlawful pushing of Blacks back into slavery through debt servitude."

— Dr. Joy DeGruy, *Post Traumatic Slave Syndrome*

Stories from an interview with my 85-year-old aunt describing this era left me in awe. "Growing up, we worked the fields together picking cotton and strawberries up in Marshall, Arkansas. As we got older Daddy would pay us 50 cents for 400 pounds of cotton. One time, my sister got bit by a snake in a strawberry field up in Missouri, they rushed her to the hospital. We stayed in the field. We would cut wood because there weren't any boys; so, we did the work of boys."

It's impossible to grasp the tremendous resiliency of the mothers in our stories without considering the cruel and harsh realities of the era in which they were born. We knew that walking the delicate balance of learning their history without reliving the trauma was probably not possible. Therefore, we prayed together each week and before each assignment. I was upfront and transparent from the beginning about seeking The Holy Spirit to guide us in every phase of the project. I was intentional in our Spirit-led approach of using scripture, writing prompts, activities, and conversations to help us to convey our mothers' real stories, careful to stay close to the guideposts of love, redemption, and reconciliation. Finding healing, forgiveness, grace, and a God-inspired resolve continues to be our prayer for ourselves and our readers.

MY WRITING ASSIGNMENT FROM GOD.

> *"I will stand at my guard post and station myself on the ramparts. I will watch to see what He will say to me, and how I should answer when corrected. 2Then the LORD answered me: "Write down this vision and clearly inscribe it on tablets, so that a herald may run with it. 3For the vision awaits an appointed time; it testifies of the end and does not lie. Though it lingers, wait for it, since it will surely come and will not delay."*
> — Habakkuk 2:2-4 ESV

My prophesied assignment comes from the pen of the prophet Isaiah's 58th chapter. The English Standard Version (ESV) Bible records the 12th verse of that chapter this way,

> *"And your ancient ruins shall be **rebuilt**;*
> *you shall **raise up** the foundations of many generations;*
> *you shall be called the **repairer** of the breach,*
> *the **restorer** of streets to dwell in."*

To gain a deeper understanding of my I assignment, specific to the writing of this book, I used the Blue Letter Bible to define the ancient meanings of each of the four points in this 12th verse.

1. REBUILD the ancient ruins (establish, cause to continue)
   Their legacy continues. Through the act of writing our mothers' stories against the backdrop of the trials of their history — we established a covenant with God's Word past, present, and future.

2. RAISE UP the foundations (arise, stand, rouse, stir up, investigate, establish, bring on the scene). *With imagination and poetic justice, we stirred up and brought on the scene a beautiful plot twist of our mothers' struggles and triumphs.*

3. REPAIRER of the breech (close up, fence up, hedge, make up (a wall), mason) *Our words carried the power of a rock mason, hedging and closing up gaps in our understanding, thereby repairing the breech between author and mother.*

4. RESTORER of paths (to return, turn back, to bring back, refresh, repair, allow to return, put back, draw back, give back, relinquish, give in payment.) *Perhaps the most rewarding to each of us as authors was this gift of giving grace to reframe their stories in love, admiration, and honor. Gifted with the miracle of the pen to bring into vision the invisible thoughts of God, I find joy in making the vision clear even as I gaze at the painful wounds of what was, through the cleansed lens of revelation, regeneration, restoration, and rebuilding that only comes from Our Father.*

THE POWER OF STORYTELLING TO HEAL, RESTORE AND REPAIR.

> *When the brain sees or hears a story, its neurons fire in the same patterns as the speaker's brain. This is known as neural coupling. "Mirror neurons" create coherence between a speaker's brain and the brains of his/her audience members.*
> — arielgroup.com

Neuroscience has given us a powerful glimpse into how storytelling synchronizes the brain of the storyteller to the brain of the listener. Known as neural coupling, the brain's neurons fire in the same patterns as the speaker's brain as they tell the story. I posit with my sanctified imagination that an even more powerful connection occurs as a child seeks to see her mother through the lens of love, honor and legacy. The ability to see her mother, gazing back at her, "mirroring neurons" of love exchanging understanding, mercy and grace. What a fulfilling reward for the writers of this collaboration to receive connection and miraculous transformation – for committing to share the stories of our mothers.

THE IMPORTANCE OF TELLING STORIES FROM OUR PAINFUL PAST

"Telling our stories can be redemptive. Telling our stories can free us. Telling our stories can lift others up. I believe an integral part of racial socialization is learning the history of those in our family and community. Storytelling is an important part of our education; it strengthens us and helps us build resilience. It helps us put things in the proper perspective. Why don't we do more of it? I believe two things tend to get in the way of African Americans telling their own stories and those about their parents and their parents' parents. I remember hearing a Jewish woman say, "surviving has not looked pretty," for many who have been oppressed.

It is clear that surviving and struggling as African Americans has often meant enduring tremendously demeaning and humiliating situations, remember as shameful episodes not to be acknowledged or discussed. In efforts to move beyond the humiliation from past injustices, many of us have disassociated ourselves from indignities our relatives experienced in the struggle to prevail over slavery, systemic racist practices, and poverty. Our failure to pass along these accounts of our familial past becomes a detriment to ourselves and our children. Within the stories lie the missing pieces of information that help us understand who we are today."

— Dr. Joy DeGruy, author, Post Traumatic Slave Syndrome: America's Legacy of Enduring Injury & Healing

STORIES ABOUT MAMA

WRITING AS THE KINGDOM BRIDGE, CONNECTING AND RECORDER

> *"[17] For the kingdom of God is not a matter of eating and drinking, but of righteousness, peace and joy in The Holy Spirit, [18] because anyone who serves Christ in this way is pleasing to God and receives human approval.[19] Let us therefore make every effort to do what leads to peace and to mutual edification."*
> — Romans 14:17-19 (NIV).

This type of writing is spiritually, emotionally, and intellectually connecting. Writing about our mothers, reconnects us at a spiritual level – as we communicate with and through Holy Spirit with the goal of seeking understanding, peace, mutual respect, and admiration. Writing2Heal serves as a compassionate recorder for our lives, giving us a historical marker to which we can refer, extending an invitation to heal together, rooted in love.

It's about restoring our mamas to the place of honor that God originally gave. Black women were not acknowledged, celebrated, or respected. Yet, the very things they were denied they poured into their children and others! This is the story of each of the women honored in this book. Many of our Black mothers were silenced, throughout their lives, and so I make no apologies for taking this opportunity to tell their stories through a lens of honor. Compelled, we must tell our mothers' stories, boldly, vulnerably, and transparently without the silencing and rejection that they surely faced. We have the freedom to speak for them, with grateful understanding of the Kingdom descriptor given in Romans 14 – in righteousness, peace, and joy. Because our mothers lived in and through an unprecedented era that forced them into characterizations that did not tell the whole story of who they were, the authors in this collaboration beautifully take license to introduce another point of view – one that accentuates the positive.

Unfortunately, many children of Black mothers who felt the harshness and disregard of the era they were born into, did not or could not know the stories of nor see the fullness of who their mothers - these fierce Black women - really were. We could only view her through young eyes receiving all the love and wisdom she could give from her experience. And yes, sometimes abuse, neglect, and ill-advice poured from the broken vessel we knew as mama. She could only give from that place. We may not have understood that before - but we understand it now.

HEALING – RAISE UP THE FOUNDATION OF MANY GENERATIONS

Our intention and purpose in writing this book is the healing of Black women from the wounds we have regarding our mothers. Far too many Black women have never purposely engaged in healing; seeking to understand our mothers in full context of the time and seasons of life. To provide a gracious space to look beyond the pain and the shame of their mothers' stories and honor her by seeing her through the lens of grace and glory. It is critical that we consider the sum of everything that they have gone through to see what incredible super women they are. In doing so, we rewrite the narrative about the Black woman in America.

The original call for authors was for women of color who have either lost their mothers, didn't have the greatest relationship with them, or who had/have magnificent moms. Healing, reconciliation, and acknowledgment of the need for personal self-development and growth, were all fruit produced as the stories emerged. We called on women who wanted to heal, to practice the Word of God, and to, "Honor thy father and mother; (which is the first commandment with promise;)" Ephesians 6:2. We called on women to help restore their mothers' legacies by reframing the narrative of precious (sometimes painful) memories into hope.

Aware that many relationships with mothers were wrapped in the pain of abuse, violence, the dysfunction of substance abuse or mental illness, or even non-existent; this reframing process is about healing for the writers (and readers) regardless of the relationship.

REPARATION THROUGH IMAGINATION

OUR WRITE2HEAL PROCESS

In co-creating our stories with the intention of honoring our mothers in our writing, we were activated to actively demonstrate the responses to critical questions.

What would your mother want you to write about her?
How did she change over the years?
If she had the opportunity to relive her life, what would she have changed?
What do I think my mother would change if she had the opportunity?
What do you think about the era in which she lived?
What if our stories were the bridge to bring reconciliation between the past and present?

How can you walk out Ephesians 6:2?
How do you honor when you ask the questions to uncover her story?
How can I honor someone who has dishonored me?
How can I honor someone that abused me?
How can I honor someone who neglected me?

In addressing our relationships, we also had to write a love letter either to or from our mothers, as an expression of love, and a method of finding gratitude for her.

In answering these questions – many of us found that we could see ourselves in our mothers – making it less likely to judge standing in her shoes. Some of us are now mothers ourselves. We don't want to be measured by the same measuring stick that we used for our own mothers.

As a Black mother myself, I find it exceptionally important to be explicit in my intention to tell the stories of our/my mother (s), to magnify the voices of our Black mamas, through the lens of love, compassion, understanding, and life.

This group of courageous women (and one brave man) who are telling their mother stories have been transformed through this Write2Heal process. You hear it in their voices. You see it in their writing, where they may have started this process with anger, bitterness, misunderstanding, and confusion – or simply had questions – now humbly blessed to have the opportunity to share beautiful *Stories About Mama*!

"I am certain that I missed out on the most incredible insight, conversations and stories from my mother because I was too busy trying to make her fit into a mold for which she was not created. I have grown to appreciate how uniquely different my mother was. I've grown to appreciate the courage and bold tenacity that she possessed to simply be herself."

Margie (Marching) to the Beat of a Different Dreamer

Written in Honor and Loving Memory of Margie Lee Dooley
AUTHOR: DR. KAREN MAXFIELD-LUNKIN

"Why should we be in such desperate haste to succeed and
in such desperate enterprises? If a man does not keep
pace with his companions, perhaps it is because he hears
a different drummer. Let him step to the music which he
hears, however measured or far away."
— Henry David Thoreau

The stories about *my* Mama are uniquely paradoxical as she was. Rough around the edges, yet such rare beauty and strength; lighthearted, yet as volatile as summer storm; delightfully funny, yet stubborn as a persistent stream following a rainstorm; crafty, creative and confident, yet self-conscious and self-doubting. Many of my memories are not pretty stories, easy to tell, but my truth, nonetheless.

Her truth.

The amount of shame that I developed surrounding "growing up with Margie" and carried well into adulthood, I know now was more about me and how I wanted to be perceived by the world. My Mama lived life on her own terms and refused to conform. Even at her death, I could sense my Mama leaving everyone to grapple with what they thought of her as their own business, that they would have to reconcile on their own terms. Yeah, she wanted to be cremated!

A KNACK FOR THE ELEMENT OF SURPRISE

When Mama died, we had her cremated (per her wishes from as long as we could remember), she always told us when we were younger that when she died, she wanted to be cremated and to have her ashes spread on the beautiful foothills of Arkansas. We also spread them near her favorite fishing spot.

Oh, the looks and curious stares as folks filed into the funeral of this small, missionary Black Baptist church to see a beautiful, green urn centered where a casket would be, flanked by flowers and a photograph of my mother. In hindsight, the stares may not have been as intense as I perceived as much as the intensity of my own insecurities surrounding how my mother (and I) were viewed. I was always worried about what other folks thought. And we butted heads over that for sure. I know Mama was looking down, loving every, talk-of-the-town-unlike-anything-ever-seen moment of it!

AN ABSOLUTE AND TIMELESS BEAUTY

Memories of staring at my mother as she dressed to go out on the town, later mimicking her pointed toed high heeled shoes, she was truly one of the most beautiful women that I've ever seen. Her beauty was in the eye of many who beheld her, not just her daughter. My dad was madly in love with her, often kissing her in public to the point that she would beg him to stop. They married and divorce twice by the time I was four years old, although they both remarried and went on to live their lives apart, they never really seemed to get over each other. My Dad even proclaimed the source of how she broke his heart just days before his death as he lay in the hospital. Margie truly marched to the beat of a different "dreamer."

THE SHAME AND SHAMBLES OF LIVING WITH MENTAL ILLNESS
THE TRUTH IS IN THE TRAUMA –

When the truth is in the trauma, it's often difficult to tell the story. Sometimes called, "running from the text", I have experienced this phenomenon on more than one occasion.

Writing my mother's story is one of those times. I asked myself a myriad of questions: How much do I tell and how much do I conceal? What will people think of me, knowing that my relationship with my mother was painfully dysfunctional at best? Should I just omit my mother's story altogether and focus on the other authors? Should I just simply write a poem? Or do I persist, just as my mother would and tell my story, her story, our story – the truth and set our spirits free?

The scripture says, "You will know the truth and the truth will set you free." In my case and often in my life, I have run from the truth by attempting to alter it, ignore it or completely sidestep it. How many people miss out on this type of freedom wasting time, energy, creativity and life trying to alter the narrative – trying to fit into a reality that we *think* is better than our own?

WHAT GOES ON IN THIS HOUSE, STAYS IN THIS HOUSE

My mama was fiercely independent and consequently had to carry the weight of her pain, alone.

Mama so desperately wanted her family to be together – however, the trauma she lived and caused was too heavy for her to bear – so she pretended it didn't happen. I remember being confused and later downright angry as she described our "perfect little family" to friends and extended family. Mama did not know how to acknowledge the trauma, make amends, and move on. Since becoming a mother myself, I understand. Deep cuts the wounds a mother inflicts upon her children herself – and the saying is true, "hurt people hurt people." This mother can never stand in judgment of another mother. For it's only by God's grace that my children survived me!

I cannot tell my mother's story without sharing the tremendous heartache that existed between us. In my young years, I fought to understand the struggle she allowed us to be in, especially since my dad lived in the same city. I compared our lack of resources to our other cousins, on both sides of my family. I felt as if we were second-rate citizens even among our own family. But it was my mother's incredible determination to be on her own that often led us to places of hunger, abandonment, and misunderstanding. There were multiple days where there was no electricity or running water in our double-wide trailer. I remember my mother being depressed and crying on her bed; and I also remember her getting up and doggedly going to work. From mood swings, extreme anger, to depression and then wonderful playfulness and boisterous laughter – Mom randomly ran the gamut. I did not know or understand growing up, that she was showing the classic signs of bipolar illness. I know for certain that if the authorities had gotten involved, we would have been taken from her. Thus, we had been well-coached about not talking. I can still hear my Mama saying, "Don't you go out this house talking about what goes on in here." Not talking was the worst thing we could have done - because she did not receive the help that she needed. Everything she experienced was then passed down to us.

Much of what Black families have endured needs to be expressed, discussed, examined and released! There is no shame in seeking therapy for the traumas we have endured.

Post Traumatic Slave Syndrome (P.T.S.S.) is a theory that explains the etiology of many of the adaptive survival behaviors in African American communities throughout the United States and the Diaspora. It is a condition that exists as a consequence of multigenerational oppression of Africans and their descendants resulting from centuries of chattel slavery. A form of slavery

STORIES ABOUT MAMA

which was predicated on the belief that African Americans were inherently/genetically inferior to whites. This was then followed by institutionalized racism which continues to perpetuate. ~ Dr Joy DeGruy, author of Post Traumatic Slave Syndrome injury.

HER-STORY, A GLIMPSE INTO MAMA'S BEGINNINGS

As the bus drove down that dusty, curvy road to Pine Street High School, Margie quickly changed out of her skirt into a pair of shorts.

"Margie, you're going to get us in trouble. I'm going to get a whoopin' when we get home."

In the mid 1950's, Annie Dooley, my grandma, required her girls to wear dresses to school - even to play sports. This trip was no exception.

"I ain't wearing no skirt to play basketball, hear?"

My aunt laughed and shook her head as she recalled the story.

"That's what she said while she was putting those shorts on, knowing full well that we were not allowed to wear pants – I still see her looking back at me mischievously."

"What they don't know, won't hurt them." Margie quipped, "And a whoopin' only lasts so long!" Aunt Mae laughed out loud as she recalled my mama's boldness.

I could hear the amusement in her voice as my aunt went on to describe how she remembered that my mama always seemed to get her way as they were growing up. She was charismatic and persuasive.

Getting this glimpse into my Mama's early life brought some clarity to this incredibly complex woman – regal beauty and stature, yet so "down home" personality that made everyone feel included, with that infectious sense of humor. On the flip side, she was equally as violent and volatile in temperament when she felt slighted or disrespected in any way. That temper could flair in a moment, with little warning.

BEAUTY SCARRED BY AN UGLY ERA

It is apparent that my Mama lived the rest of her years rebelling against what she deemed as strict and unreasonable rules of the time. While Margie was energetic, funny and friendly, she had a side to her that often scared me. She would quickly flare up in anger whenever she perceived a spirit of racism or a hint of condescension from white people. She detested having ever cleaned houses for white people or to accept the idea that Black people were inferior to whites. My Mama was in many ways ahead of her time. She developed a sense of humor that I now understand was a way to deflect the deep wounds inflicted from this deeply racist and misogynistic era in which she lived.

My aunt continued reflecting on who my mom was, "I remember her as someone who always got her way." I agreed. That is the Margie (Mama) I knew as a little girl. I remember her as a fierce presence with an insatiable sense of humor. She could, however, go into a rage that shook the sides of our trailer home. The quote by Eleanor Roosevelt, that "well behaved women seldom make history" completely captures my mother.

I often try to imagine what it was like to be young, gifted, fierce, woman and Black during the decades between 1940 and 1960. I mean dealing with that triple consciousness of being a brilliant woman, and a Black visionary, still trying to identify as African and American.

Born seventh of 15 children in 1938, in the foothills of the Ozarks in a small community known as Solomon Grove, Arkansas, she was an absolute beauty queen.

Because she was creative, free willed, stubborn, and determined, I often wonder how she survived during such a racist and misogynistic era. Although she did give me insight into what life was like in the rural south in the dawn of the Civil Rights Movement. I honestly believe that the wild way that she lived - free and on her own terms - was related to her upbringing. The type of upbringing that could crush or inspire a young Black, beautiful woman raised in the south during Jim Crow and before the Civil Rights Movement.

CREATIVITY – GENIUS

A HORSE OF A DIFFERENT COLOR

My mother was a maverick in many ways - beautiful and strong but refused to follow the rules or to be tamed. She dreamed differently and faced the inequities of her day differently.

When my parents divorced (for the second time), my mother moved from Denver to Boulder, Colorado. As I grew older, I recognized that she was exposing us, as much as she could, to a different culture. Running as far away from the country hills and memories of picking cotton and strawberries without a choice in the matter. It was as if we were turning our backs on our roots and reaching for something completely different. There were many times when we were the only Black children in all White schools. I had definite bouts with identity crisis growing up. It was my mother's way of escaping and making sure we were not exposed to the race schisms of the south. Although we traveled to Arkansas almost every summer, and some summers stayed the entire time with my grandparents, mom still found it important for us to live up north.

I still see her striving to be heard, accepted, and even celebrated for who she was. I often say that she was a woman born before her time, because she was a thought leader, a visionary and one who bucked the systems. She did that even if it meant breaking the law. My beautiful mother was "something else." While some may frown on this, my first smoke of marijuana was with my mother and her good friend (who also smoked with her children). My first and only sip of her favorite scotch, Chivas Regal, was with my mother. Oh, did I mention these were before I was 10 years old?

She was so determined to live life on her own terms that there were times we struggled financially. We sometimes lived well-below poverty; but she would not ask for help. She wanted the image of success and abundance to us. And it worked for a while; but there came a breaking point in our lives. There were many times when she would leave my sister, brother, and me at home alone. Were we latchkey kids, neglected or abused? It depends on with whom you spoke. But I called it a young, Black, single mother doing what she knew to make ends meet.

My mother was immensely proud of us, even though when we left home it was not on the best of terms. She would always brag about her children, and she would always send birthday cards to her grandchildren as soon as their month arrived. If my mother could go back and change anything in her life, I believe it would be choosing to get the help that she needed emotionally and psychologically. If she had gotten that type of help, her relationship with her children would not have been so strained.

I choose to look beyond the circumstances in which my mother raised her children. Instead, I choose to accentuate the positives: how she persevered in the face of incredible racism.; how she had an insatiable sense of humor and could hold a conversation with anyone and have them laughing within minutes. My mother was the favorite aunt among my cousins. She loved to fish and would take anyone fishing with her. It was part of her playfulness. An incredible cook, she would fish, grill, make and sell barbecue; still known as making the best fried chicken I've ever tasted. She was so brilliant.

I am certain that I missed out on the most incredible insight and conversations and stories from my mother because I was too busy trying to make her fit into a mold for which she was not created. I have grown to appreciate how unique and different my mother was. I've grown to appreciate the courage and bold tenacity that she possessed by simply being herself.

Margie to the beat of a different dreamer ... thank you for giving me the most unique perspective of life.

> *"When you finally learn that a person's behavior has more to do with their own internal struggle than you, you learn grace."*
> — Allison Aars

Marjorie Lee Dooley(left), pictured here with two of her sisters, Jewell Senior and Wanda Dooley.

"My momma mantra: Treat others the way YOU want to be treated. My momma always instilled hope and peace. She believes that time will tell a person true intent. But never get out of character to appease anyone. She always says, "You know who you are, don't let know one tell you anything different."

My Mama, the Warrior and Shero!

Written in Honor of: Fannie Earnestine Banks Garrett
AUTHOR: ANGELA TAITT

Proverbs 31:25-31 - "Strength and honor are her clothing; she shall rejoice in time to come. She opens her mouth with wisdom, and on her tongue is the law of kindness. She watches over the ways of her household and does not eat the bread of idleness. Her children rise up and call her blessed. Her husband also, and he praises her: Many daughters have done well, but you excel them all. Charm is deceitful and beauty is passing. But a woman who fears the Lord, she shall be praised. Give her the fruits of her hands, and let her own works praise her in the gates."

CHILDHOOD

My momma, the warrior and shero, Fannie Earnestine Banks Garrett, was born to tobacco sharecroppers Sam and Elizabeth Foushee Banks, January 21, 1949. In Vine Grove, Kentucky. Dr. Miller delivered her in good health. My momma was named after a married couple, Fannie and Earnestine, for whom her mother and father worked. Early on, her father gave her the nickname Butterball because she was as round as a turkey.

My momma was forced to do chores typically relegated to men

during that time, but she did not mind doing. She learned to drive a tractor and loved to hang out with her dad. The youngest of the girls but the oldest of the three boys. My momma had few responsibilities in the house, and her childhood was full of love and challenges.

SCHOOL DAYS

While Momma loved going to school, first through fifth grade. Kentucky in the 50's were taught in a segregated manner at Zion Grove School. The school was housed in a church.called Zion Grove, where various speakers on Saturdays and Sundays would hold Sunday school and worship services. My momma would be escorted to services by Bernice Foushee, her grandfather.

In an interesting turn of events, education officials decided that the Black teachers at Zion Grove and other schools in the area were not qualified to teach. The school system ordered that all the Black schools be shut down, Black students were then forced to attend an all-White Catholic school from sixth through eighth grade. In that environment, they had no choice but to study Catholicism. She recalls being confused by their tenets because of the faith she had learned at Zion Grove. Her older siblings did not have to attend school with her and by the time the boys were enrolled, the school system was completely integrated.

Momma's older school years were filled with the excitement of changing classes and learning a variety of new subjects. There was also the excitement of seeing the country moving through the pivotal period of the 1960s. She remembers those tough times and being uncertain about whether Rev. Dr. Martin Luther King Jr. was helping or hurting Black people with the escalation of The Civil Rights Movement.

Racial differences evident around the country would also surface on school trips. In one class, she was required to go to the local skating rink, (other Black students were signed up for other outings).

She rode the bus to the skating rink with the other students, but the owner refused her the right to skate because she was Black. She did say, almost sorrowful, that he did graciously allow her to use the restroom. She would sit and watch other students skate, and then board the bus for the ride home only to be reminded of racial differences again. When the teacher would stop for ice cream, Momma would have to go to the side marked COLOREDS' ONLY. For two years, it was the same thing weekly, although the teacher was always pleasant and would pay for her ice cream as well. My momma still jokes, "That's probably why I can't skate now."

Her racial challenges were also evident on the bus rides to and from school daily. The kids would ridicule and belittle her and hurl insults at her. She would ask the bus driver for help, but he did nothing. She was a poor country girl, who saw no color, unlike those around her. All she knew about was working hard. Her white friends in the country, who experienced the hard work she did, felt the same as her. Making it back home each day gave her comfort and peace.

One afternoon, while with her friends, Martha, and Janie, she spotted a blue and white 1957 Chevy. The owner was asking six hundred dollars for it. She went home and spoke to her father about buying the car. She wanted to fight back against what she was experiencing on the bus. While my grandfather convinced her that trying to hurt them would only provoke the problem and was not worth it, he did buy the car. She had to work hard to repay the investment her dad made. She did so by helping her grandmother, Margaret Foushee (Wawa as she was known) clean houses.

During her 11th and 12th grade years she was allowed to drive to church and to school. Having her own car proved beneficial when she joined the track team. The embarrassment and humiliation of taking her clothes off to shower for the first time was too much. She was able to drive herself away from that torment. My mother graduated from high school in 1967, with a class of 360 students. She kept working as a housekeeper and babysitting to earn money, since college, at the time, was out of the question.

BEING A YOUNG ADULT

By the time she was 19, Momma would meet and marry my father, John Henry Garrett. She and dad met on a blind date. He was a friend of her sister's date. Shortly after they were married on March 9, 1968, Momma became pregnant with me - Angela Sue Garrett -Taitt. I was born September 13th of that same year. My mother wanted to marry my dad because he was a U.S. Army Sergeant and was being deployed to Vietnam. There was no certainty, and little hope that he would make it back. While he was deployed, she – a pregnant newlywed - lived with her parents. Against all odds, dad did come home in 1969.

My sister, Sherrell Denise Garrett, was born on July 5, 1972. Our young military family then moved to Panama, where Momma focused on raising my sister and me. During our time there, she taught us how to swim, and we enjoyed outdoor activities together. She was very hands-on; but she also allowed us to be kids, who were well-disciplined when needed. Since she was a talented seamstress, she always made our clothes (dressing me and my sister like twins). My dad would teach her how to make things from scratch, and we would benefit from whatever she learned. Moving back stateside, my parents bought a house, though we would be stationed at various places, including Ft. Campbell, Kentucky, Ft. Bragg, North Carolina., Germany, and Ft. Hood, Texas. My dad often had solo assignment orders; those would take him to Korea, Honduras, and other foreign places.

PRECIOUS MEMORIES

Momma loved her family; and because of this, she taught us to love people regardless of how they treat you, or how much money you have. She always says, "Do not treat people differently because in the end love always wins." It was that teaching, and her direction to stand up for ourselves that inspired my degree in social work. She believes that you can do anything you put your mind to. To prove that my mother played softball (a game she loves) until she was 35, and the doctor forced her to stop. Momma played softball for over twenty years. When I was seven, she was playing in a game. She slid into home plate, then threw the ball all the way to the outfield. She never let gender, age, or other people's restrictions stop her. I wanted to be just like her.

I recall how memorable my 13th birthday party was in North Carolina. I got disco skates and skated all down the streets with my friends. If you were looking for me, you would find me at the skating rink with my friends. I became a great skater! It was during that time; Momma shared her traumatic skating story with me. Then there was my 16th birthday. She rented a community center on Ft. Hood, and half the city attended. I had to stand at the door and turn people away.

My momma made certain holidays memorable. Our Christmas celebrations were epic. What others did not see often was her patriotism. She loved celebrating at the different military parades and holding up signs applauding and recognizing troops on their return home. No one saw her silent battles; but she lived a powerful prayer life (and still does). She made certain that we attended church faithfully. Momma did not allow us to fall asleep in church, nor did she allow us to go to children's church. We would walk in and leave together. Following her example, my dad began to join us in worship and became faithful to the ministry. With this example this allowed me to be and serve in ministry in my later years.

NO-NONSENSE ONE-OF-A-KIND

My momma has a one-of-a-kind personality; and part of that personality is giving. She will give you the shirt off her back, my sister may say. She is extremely likable and does not meet strangers. She meets lifelong friends. She loves clothes and fashion. One thing one would surely know about my momma is that whatever color outfit she is wearing, her accessories (hat, jewelry, and shoes) will match. And between you and me, even her undergarments will match. I would take advantage of her fashion sense and sewing skills during high school. Once I asked her to make a unique outfit for me. I even convinced her to make matching outfits for me and my guy friend once. She loved doing it, and I loved watching and helping. After high school, I enrolled in a fashion design school – guess who stepped in when my final project needed completing?

Momma is a bit obsessive compulsive when it comes to her wardrobe. She keeps an extra pair of shoes in her car in case she gets anything on the pair she's wearing for the day. Yet, she will have a yard sale with everything, including clothing, selling for $1.00; and anything left over she readily donates.

One of the funniest things she has ever taught me was, "Don't ever let a man tell you that you can't drive a sports car because guess what, I taught you how to." The funny thing is she's driven various types of cars, including a sports car, since I was in middle school. When my dad played tennis, racquetball, and golf, she was determined to learn each game just to beat him.

Professionally she worked as a teacher for over 20 years. After retiring, she decided to broaden her horizon and earned two Associate Degrees in Human Services and Early Childhood Development, and a bachelor's in business management. An intelligence powerhouse, she maintained a 4.0 grade point average at both levels. She then re-entered the workforce as Assistant Director of the Childcare Center at Ft. Campbell, Kentucky. She was promoted to Childcare

Director and held that position for six years before full retirement. My father, who was promoted to a Military Army Chief Warrant Officer, retired in 1993. He and Momma have been married for more than five decades. My mother joyfully spends her days with my dad, though you can often find her hiding in her she-shed or hanging out and visiting with her siblings.

THE EPITOME OF A WARRIOR!

My mom is the epitome of a warrior, defending her core feminine values, standing up for others, and defending children's rights. Whatever role she is serving in, she achieves greatness by standing her ground and pushing for change. My momma is my shero, my rock, my solace. Her story is one of resilience, persistence, love, and compassion. Even though I can't tell it all she is a warrior. Even now, there are times I call with a problem, and she may not have the answers, but she is always present and available.

I thank God for the legacy and the past that has made her who she is today and for her profound imprint in my life. May God pour out more blessing upon her, and continue the legacy given to us. I am sure my sister would attest to that; and I am certain her five grandchildren (Ravin, Tiffany, Michael, Rashai, and Robert Jr.) and her four great-grandchildren (Asha, Rylie, Aila and A'mriss) feel the same.

Co-author Angela Taitt's mother, Fannie Earnestine Banks Garrett

"Our princess parties turned to prayer meetings. We weren't just going to church; we were bringing church home with us. Our fairy tale life became one big hallelujah revival."

A Mother Is Your First Friend, Best Friend, Forever Friend

Written in Honor of: Josephine Lee Phillips
AUTHOR: FELECIA KAMBERLY ROSE

They say that a girl's mother is her first best friend. As a preteen, that sentiment only rang true for me in movies and sitcoms about white girls who lived in two-story houses. Scenes come to mind of Little Suzie telling Mother about her day and the boy she hopes will ask her out. Then Mom and Suzie talk about the upcoming dance over milk and cookies. All is well and right in their world. That's what I was led to think mother and daughter relationships were. Little Suzie, however, didn't look like me and my relationship with my mother was never what I saw on television.

Don't get me wrong, Mama was a good mom by real-world standards. Still, I wanted June Cleaver from the TV show "Leave it to Beaver" suburban goodness. I wanted a mom who didn't yell, and problems that were solved in 30 minutes or less. I mean, we baked cookies, but they were usually to give away. Our talks about boys sounded like this, "Go sit your tail down and don't ever let anybody touch you down there!" I didn't get the luxury of having my mom as a best friend. My mom was too busy preparing me for the real world and all its heartbreaks to be my little friend. She had to be so much more.

Mama was a chameleon. She would go from being my mother to

being the favorite auntie or the favorite teacher or Jesus's favorite first cousin (as we hilariously refer to her). She became who and what the situation warranted. Mama was the epitome of all things amazing. Everybody loved my mama; and if they didn't, it wasn't any fault of her own. Anyone who had the privilege of being in her presence left with something, whether it was a slice of her magnificently moist pound cake, or a soul-stirring, tear-jerking prayer. We were fed, clothed, educated, and knew the Lord. What more could a kid ask for? People had no problem letting me know that I was blessed to have such a wonderful mom. My mama was everybody's everything; so, I quickly made peace with her belonging to everybody else.

It wasn't always this way. Before the world knew how awesome she was, and before I knew how cruel the world could be, she solely belonged to me and my sister. Our early days rivaled a magical, brown-sugared fairy tale. Our summers were legendary; filled with breakfasts in bed, pretty princess tea parties in the yard and bags full of library books. It was the best life ever; until things changed. My mama changed, and our reality forcibly did the same. She ascended to a substantially higher level in her relationship with God and never looked back. She began living, breathing, and eating all things Godly. Our princess parties turned to prayer meetings. We weren't just going to church; we were bringing church home with us. Our fairy tale life became one big hallelujah revival. Summers once spent in laughter were spent in praise and worship and holy shouting.

One summer afternoon Mama informed us there would be no more TV until we got the Holy Ghost, which meant we would be overwhelmed in the being and presence of God perpetually. To get this indwelling, we had to kneel on pillows for hours screaming aloud, "Jesus. Jesus., Jesus!" I asked God to help me catch the Holy Ghost, so she would leave me alone and let me watch my show. He answered my prayer because my incessant stuttering resembled whatever she needed it to, and she set me free. That summer would begin a journey of religious and denominational experimentation. We went from

34

Baptist to African to a cult or two in between. We experienced every denomination except the infamous Church Of God In Christ. I don't know how we missed that one.

We traveled all over our home state of Mississippi looking for Jesus. He was quite elusive. Some days Mama found everything but Jesus. There was the crazy pastor's wife who came to fight her. There was the cult leader who made us wear layers of clothing down to the floor. We were always trapped on her adventures. There would be times I would see things happening and ask God to show her what I saw before something even crazier happened. He would grant my prayer, and we would be on to the next stop. She would get hurt and knocked down, but never for long. Those adventures taught me how to know where God wasn't, and how to pray until He showed up. I loathed that part of my mother's story, yet it shaped my own. I am grateful she never gave up on God.

THAT'S JUST THE WAY THINGS WERE

Josephine Lee was born on the first day of spring, smack dab in the middle of Equen Plantation in Minter City, Mississippi, the fourth of 11 siblings She chopped cotton as a child and wasn't allowed to start the school year until everything was harvested. All the money earned went to the family budget; but her father would give her spending money. During the school year, she would go to school in the day, babysit at night, sleep, then rise to do it all over again.

Sundays were different. On Sunday nights, her father would come home full of liquid courage and colorful language. No one ever knew why this was his routine. He would be so full of rage that any conversation could escalate to violence, supported by his gun. They would have to run for their lives. She and her mama were always the first to get out. She vividly remembers jumping over bales of hay, bullets zooming by her ear. Their hiding places would vary between the homes of others on the plantation. These homes belonged to women who understood the uncertainty and volatility of weekend liquor binging. She would spend those Sunday nights wondering if the others made it out alive. On Monday mornings, they would return home and get dressed for school like nothing happened. They never talked about it. She would spend the bulk of her adult years making sure everybody was okay, including her father. Every decision she made as an adult was centered around her love for her family, from the car she drove to how she spent her days off. Family over everything - including her.

One gloomy Saturday morning, I was harassing my legally blind mama via text messaging to answer her ringing phone. "Girl answer, I have questions!"

She calls, sensing something is up. I weasel my way through icebreakers to peak into her past. "Mama, what's your favorite color?"

"Blue," she answers.

I ask incredulously, "Which one?"

She yells, "Red! Since you want to be difficult."

She's on to me. I can hear it in her voice. She suffers through more small talk as we weave through a lightning round of fun facts. I ask her if she has a favorite sibling. She responds as if I have blasphemed the name of the Lord. "No, that wouldn't be fair to anybody. They're all great in their own right." She's protective of them, still.

We talk about her favorite childhood memories. The doll she didn't expect to get on her sixth birthday. The time they got real cereal bowls, and no longer had to use the tin ones. Simple things my sister and I took for granted. I tiptoe toward the heavier questions. Stories I already know but want to hear again through more appreciative ears. I open up Pandora's Box of Mama-do-you-remember questions. She remembers, though she would like to forget.

We navigate through memories until the air becomes too thick to giggle through. We talked about how her big brother whisked her away from her menial life in Minter City and her short-lived life in St. Louis. Although she grew up in church, St. Louis was her first real glimpse of God. After a week of fasting for the first time, she had a vision of another brother lying in a funeral home she was passing by. Days later, he would tragically pass away. She would go home for his funeral and never look back. She was fortunate enough to get a job working with her mother; eventually becoming the cafeteria manager. She would meet my father, a teacher, in that cafeteria. She didn't like him because he was always asking for more food. He would beg and she would eventually relent. They began a relationship that would lead to marriage. He encouraged her to go back to school. She would finally become the teacher everyone always told her she should be. People told her they knew that was what she was supposed to be because of her eyebrows. They said with her type of eyebrows she would either go crazy or be a teacher. Thank God for teaching. She was such a wonderful teacher, that she won teacher of the year two times.

We talk about how she lost her two biggest critics, her father and then her father-in-law in the same year, one in the spring, the other in the fall. Then her brothers, one in the spring and one in the fall. The nervous breakdowns that would follow come up in the conversation. The doctor explained that when one's body is used to going, then no longer has anywhere to go, it eventually shuts down. I ask her how long it took for her to recover. She says weeks. I say months. The reality was never. We sit in silence. I ask my mama did her father ever apologize? No, she responded. I laugh at the absurdity of it all.

"Mama," I say. "That's a lot to live through. How did you survive all those years?"

She replies, "Sometimes you forget; and sometimes you simply move on."

She repeatedly simply moved on until she forgot. And just like that, everything made sense. All of the going, all of the giving … it all made sense. I was so consumed with the fact that my mom didn't have time for me that I could not see she never had time for herself.

We forget that parents were people before children and families, and that their lives did not magically begin at our conception. Although their worlds may revolve around ours (for at least 18 years), life does not stop gunning for them. We talk some more about failed friendships, evil coworkers and how she's outlived them all.

"Mama, do you miss anything that you gave up for us?"

"Nothing at all." She replies.

I giggle because there's got to be something. She stands her ground. I feel guilty for bringing up old stuff. I check on her later to see if all the questions made her sad. She's fine. I am not. My heart hurts for the life she never got to have and all the sacrifices she chose to make. I weep for all the times she had to move on without apology or resolution. I had been so unfair all these years. How do I make up for lost time? I can't. I simply move on.

I get it now. I had a phenomenal mom. When she said she was doing the best that she could, she absolutely meant that. Our mother-daughter-bestie love/hate/love affair has ebbed and flowed with the best of them. I've made peace with whom we've been, and I look forward to who we are becoming. I wish my mom had given herself more and the world less, but I understand now that her giving kept her sane. It made amends for all the times she felt guilty for getting out and moving on. It was her penance. The price she paid for surviving all those Sundays. My goal is to give her better Sundays as we chase God together and find Him for real.

Co-author Felecia Kamberly Rose's mother, Josephine Lee Phillips

"Mama, no more back seat take your seat of honor!"

From the Back Seat to
the Seat of Honor

Honoring My Queen Louise Elizabeth Sanders
AUTHOR: KESHIA SANDERS

Rejection, Hurt, Disappointment, Pain, Poverty, Death, Sickness, Restoration, Healing

> *"When someone invites you to a wedding feast, do not take the place of honor, for a person more distinguished than you may have been invited. 9 If so, the host who invited both of you will come and say to you, 'Give this person your seat.' Then, humiliated, you will have to take the least important place. 10 But when you are invited, take the lowest place, so that when your host comes, he will say to you, 'Friend, move up to a better place.' Then you will be honored in the presence of all the other guests. 11 For all those who exalt themselves will be humbled, and those who humble themselves will be exalted."*
> — Luke 14:8-11 (NIV)

I remember as a little girl, sitting in the back of the church with my mom. We always sat in the back. I asked Mom during one service, "Why do we have to sit in the back? Can we sit in the front?"

She responded, "This is where I like sitting."

Kicking my feet, I said, "I cannot see from back here."

With a frustrated look on her face, she popped me on the thigh, leaned into my ear and mumbled, "If I tell you again to hush you are going to get a whipping."

I learned that day, with my thigh on fire, that sitting in the back was not that bad. Before Mom became disabled, she was active in church. Mom had a beautiful voice and sang in the choir, and she was a member of the missionary, hospitality, and pastor's aid ministries. She enjoyed serving others but preferred working quietly in the background. As I grew up, I realized I had developed so many of her traits.

Even today Mom still sits in the back of the church with her wheelchair parked against the wall, out of the way. For Mama, taking the back seat in life started at birth. That position would follow into adulthood, and her senior years. Keep your focus on her journey, you will be amazed.

Louise Elizabeth Roberts was born in 1935 (the year of The Great Depression) in a small town called Mullins, South Carolina. Within months of her birth, her parents Emory and Theretha separated, and her father left the home leaving no financial support. Two months later Theretha, being mentally and financially unstable, gave-up my mother (at only four-months-old) along with her three older siblings to their maternal grandparents. Her maternal aunt Daisy breastfed her along with her son who was three months older. Mom's grandparents, Simon and Avie Godbolt, were Southern Missionary Baptists and sharecroppers.

Her mom would come home from time to time to visit but always left again. Her father visited once a year, but never paid Mom any attention, showing favoritism to her siblings. Mom would often say, "My daddy didn't like me." I would hear the little girl in her voice when she'd say it, and it saddened me. I could not imagine feeling rejected by both parents.

My aunt Iva Mae stated that as a young girl, mom was sweet, smart, quiet, and pushed to the side. At the tender age of five, mom

STORIES ABOUT MAMA

worked in the cotton fields carrying water to the field workers. At the age of six she started school, walking three miles to get there because her grandparents lived deep in the country. Mom only earned a ninth-grade education due to her grandparents having to move to another farm to sharecrop. She picked cotton and helped her grandparents on the farm. At the age of 15 her biological mom fell ill and passed away. A few years later her grandfather died; their deaths forced her to deal with great sorrow and grief.

By the time she was 19, Mom would move to Marion, South Carolina with her grandmother, sister Nettie, and cousin Marvin. She then began working as a housekeeper and became a single parent, at 26 with the birth of my brother Dannie. Three years later, on Easter Sunday, her grandmother fell dead in the yard of her home. My mom laid beside her until medical workers removed her body. She was devastated and left feeling profoundly alone.

Mom's aunt Daisy, whom we all called Grandma, became the matriarch, and took care of Dannie. Mom began dating Lewis Sanders, the man who later became my father. She moved to Boston, Massachusetts, and stayed with her sister Nettie. Mom worked while attending nursing school. After receiving her nursing certificate, she worked in a nursing home for three years. Every week she sent money and clothes home for my brother and would visit often. When Dannie turned six and was starting school her aunt called my mom to return home, which she did. Sadly, she left her nursing certificate in Boston and never pursued nursing again. Mom dated my dad for eight years after she moved back home, and they finally married in 1968. One year later, she gave birth to my middle brother, Mario; and 11 months later she gave birth to me. Mom and Dad were opposites from diverse backgrounds. Even in her marriage, she remained that shy little girl who stood in the background.

My parents created a nice middle-class life for us, but that was shattered when my dad was in a bad accident that left him bedridden for nine months. My father could no longer work due to his disability.

Mom had to quit her job to take care of him. I was six years old at the time, but I remember our livelihood changing from comfortable to barely enough. Mom's 16-year-old niece gave birth and asked her to raise the baby. Mom was thrilled to do so, and she named the baby girl,Sherry, who would become part of our family at three-days-old.

Mom eventually got a job as a housekeeper at the hospital on the second shift. Sometimes after getting off from work, she would put our school clothes in a pillowcase or trash bag and walk to the laundromat to assure we had clean clothes for the next day. I never saw anyone so self-sacrificing. When she had to walk home from work at night, my brother Mario would walk two miles to meet her, so she was not alone. She never gave up; she had strong faith and strength. Some days she would go to work feeling defeated and even sick, but she would press forward.

At the age of 11, I had severe asthma and mom would rock me sitting on the edge of the bed until my breathing calmed down, and I fell asleep. She prayed and hummed for hours until she felt peace, and I was better. I never suffered from asthma again after I was 12. God heard mom's fervent prayers! Mom taught us to seek God first, pray without ceasing, keep the faith; and she taught us how to survive. I remember sitting on the steps of our home and telling the Lord I want to be somebody in life, and I was determined to become successful, so I could take care of my parents. Mom, as years passed, experienced a mountain of spiritual warfare, and suffered a nervous breakdown.

Mom loved and believed in her children; and supported and protected us the best she could. None of us ever gave her any trouble. My brother Mario and I were in college at the same time and Mom would send us each 20 dollars every two weeks with a little note that read, "*I don't get paid until another two weeks so make it last.*" She only earned $300.00 every two weeks, so that 40 dollars to us was sacrificial. After graduating from college, I moved to Maryland. One day, Mom called me and shared that it was a struggle for her to work. She had developed osteoarthritis in both hips, and it was painful for

STORIES ABOUT MAMA

her to stand. I immediately wrote a resignation letter for Mom to take to work, and we prayed. I promised her I would do my best to take care of her.

Despite times being hard, Mom remained a faithful and loving wife for 40 years. She had multiple challenges in her marriage, but she never gave up. I admired her tenacity in keeping her family together. While growing up we never heard our parents say I love you to each other or to us. It did not affect me until I was an adult and began learning the importance of saying I love you. We knew that they loved us by their actions. They grew up without anyone saying I love you to them, and it filtered down to us. We thought it was normal. When I discovered it was not normal, I became intentional about telling my parents I loved them. Saying it, then became contagious.

The last rejection, hurt and disappointment Mom experienced hit hard. My dad became extremely ill, and Mom tried her best to get him to go to the doctor. He would not go! I had to drive from Maryland and rush him to the hospital. Mom stayed with my dad in the hospital for a month, never leaving his side. His condition got worse, and he became angry and disrespectful to Mom. Anyone could walk in the room, and he would smile and do whatever they asked him to do; but with Mom, he shut down. Rejected in her marriage from her dying husband, how much more could she take? Dad passed away while my mom was sleeping. She was broken and in deep grief. As we prepared for my dad's funeral, she became numb and could not express any heartfelt emotions. A couple of years later, after prayer and forgiveness, she finally released the emotions she had bottled up and moved forward with her life.

Mom was a nurse at heart and took care of all her family members year after year until they would pass away. In doing so, she had forsaken her own health. She suffered a mild stroke and heart attack, and lost mobility in her legs. Depression overtook her so fiercely that she would wheel herself into a corner and face the wall for hours. This went on for months until my sister brought home a newborn, tiny puppy, named Coco. Coco would cry nonstop. Finally, the crying caught my mom's attention, and she began to operate in her nursing skills and take care of Coco. She found purpose and strength again, forcing depression to flee. Now Coco and Mom are inseparable.

Her strength and faith in full force again, she also rediscovered her voice. During a revival in Marion, SC, as the Spirit of God was moving mightily, Mom yelled out, "I want to walk!" The pastor prayed for her, and she miraculously began walking. Even after facing additional life-threatening health issues, God continued to miraculously heal her, and allowed her to be a living testimony that God is a healer. I asked my siblings to share a three-word description of Mom. Dannie described her as compassionate, resilient, and virtuous. Mario responded that she is forgiving, trustworthy and passionate. Sherry expressed that she is loving, kind, and sweet. Mom, to me, you are God-fearing, phenomenal, and courageous. I see and applaud your courageous strength and your strong faith. You have endured; You have overcome! My queen, I thank God for you and dedicate this chapter to you; take your seat of honor. No more back seat Mom! You are the head and not the tail. You are above and not beneath. I love you, Mom. May God continue to richly bless you and keep you in perfect health, peace, and prosperity.

Co- author Keshia Sanders' mother, Louise Sanders

"During the 19 years I had with Mama, her standard Augusta quote and directive that guided my life was, "BECAUSE I SAID SO!"

Mama's Favorite Words: "Because I Said So"

Written in Honor and Loving Memory of: Augusta Dooley Hunter
AUTHOR: LONNETTA ALBRIGHT

"Develop enough courage so that you can stand up for
yourself and then stand up for somebody else"
— Maya Angelou

INTRODUCTION

It's been close to 50 years since my mama passed away at 47. Though she lived a short life, she made a dynamic impact. She was not focused on success (that would have been about her) – rather she lived to make a significant difference in the world. I'm not sure that she knew that at the time.

How do I tell you about her? How do I honor her 47 years in an abbreviated manner? And why now? Though she has been gone for quite some time, she is always with me. Sometimes I hear her advice or admonishment in my head when I don't necessarily want to hear it. There are still times I wish I would have listened to the silent nudging, lessons, and memories that could have saved me from trouble and heartache.

It was the title of this book and that word **legacy** that motivated me to join this amazing collective of storytellers. Legacy can be financial, something you create, or instilled in the people you touch. Mama created a successful family. Her mentorship through words and song are what stands out for those who knew her. People who encountered her were better when they left her. She was the oldest of 17 children. After all these years, they continue to honor her at every turn, every family reunion, and whenever I see them.

The way she lived, the lessons she taught us and the family she created leave clues that I will use as I honor her and all that she represented. To introduce you to Augusta Mellanease Hunter, my mama; I ask myself what would she want me to say about her? What would she want you to know about her? One thing she continuously poured into us was believing in God and the scriptures. There's one scripture that I can quote no matter the Bible version. Mama had plaques made of this scripture that hung on the wall. She would want me to begin her story – and by extension my story with this scripture, "*In all thy ways acknowledge him and he shall direct thy paths.*" (Proverbs 3:6, KJV) It took close to 15 years for me to live my life according to that scripture.

BECAUSE I SAY SO: POWERFUL WORDS BUT...

During the 19 years I had with Mama, her standard Augusta quote and directive that guided my life was, "BECAUSE I SAY SO!" Those four words worked for me, until they didn't. From the start of my life, I trusted Mama on everything. As a little girl knowing that I was safe, cared for, and loved made it easy to do things her way, because she said so. As I got older, I felt she was trying to clone me. My siblings and I used to say that I was her practice child. She didn't know what she was doing as a new mom so "because I said so" was her go to answer. Go to church every Sunday, stop talking so much, get good grades, always hold your head high, no dating until you're 16, use your mind and be an independent thinker, respect your elders and others, and no sex before marriage. In my early teen years, she convinced me that I could get pregnant if I French kissed a boy.

She was a tall woman; proud, brave, smart, beautiful, comfortable in her own skin, loved and respected. Why wouldn't I do what she said? I even remember her telling my sisters (who were also tall) to never slump, stand up, walk straight and be proud of who you are even if you are the tallest students in your class. To this day they are beautiful, tall, proud, and courageous Black women. That's legacy.

But when Mama died, I was at a loss. How would I make decisions? How would I be able to carry out her final request of me - to help daddy raise the kids? One thing I knew for sure was that they would not accept "because I say so" from me. So, as a family we each brought our lessons from Mama to the table and figured out how we would move forward despite our broken hearts, young ages, and confusion. It became all about us. She always taught us that no matter what, we would always have each other.

ALL ABOUT US

To honor Mama is to share with you how she impacted those who she loved more than anything in the world – her family. Her baby and only son was special. Mama would frequently say, "he's my menopause baby." She died on his eighth birthday. Every year when we celebrate him, we celebrate her too. What was incredibly special about her that I will never forget is how she loved my half-sister, Lenora. I must admit to being jealous that Lenora, being six years older than me, usurped my place as Mama's oldest. But as only an amazing, God-fearing woman would do she accepted Dad's first daughter as hers. When mom took a job Lenora was our babysitter, and I would behave because Mama said so.

Daddy, who never remarried, was with us for a much longer time. He was 94 when he passed away. They had a strong union. As I got older, Dad would share stories about her that only demonstrated the impact she had in his life. I remember a couple of Sundays after she'd passed away, we thought we'd sleep in. Dad woke us up and asked, "What do you think you're doing"? Your mother always made you go to Sunday School, and you are going! So, get up and get ready!" Again, "because I said so" spoke into our lives.

MAMA'S KIDS & MY GIFTS

One of the biggest impacts she had on my life was the gift of my siblings. They are my best friends.

Mama brought three girls and one boy into this world. For me Lonnie was a profound gift. Not having any children of my own I had the honor and privilege to serve in a maternal role for him. So many lessons I learned from Mama helped me to nurture him.

I cannot honor her legacy without including them. So, I asked my three siblings (Lenora passed away in 2021) to help describe her impact and legacy.

THROUGH THE EYES AND HEARTS OF HER CHILDREN

1.   How would you describe Mama?

Denise – She was strong, serious, faithful, proud, no nonsense, resourceful (she even made our clothes). She took her role as wife, mother, gospel singer and woman of God to heart.

Cherie – A woman of faith, devoted to her family. A willful and audacious woman. Strong, Serious, yet playful, and a disciplinarian. A woman full of spirit.

Lonnie – A woman of virtue, talent, determination, and stature. I loved the way she took care of me, her house, the way she carried herself; and I can only imagine what home would have been like without her. Her impact was like none other.

2. What's one thing Mama shared with you that impacted your life?

Denise – "No matter how successful you become, don't ever get to a place where you think too highly of yourself." Before she died, she said that she worried about me because I was like her. I have taken both statements to heart (in both positive and negative ways).

Cherie – "Don't think too highly of yourself. Don't place any pastor, deacon, or psalmist on a pedestal; for they will inevitably disappoint you." She taught me how to cook and care for a home.

Lonnie – When I was eight, I repeated something I overheard said about someone, to that person. She said people are more important than we give them credit for. I got in trouble, but the lesson shaped how I treat people. She said, "Your testimony doesn't start until the song is over. Make sure you treat people right." Today my job is people, influencing them, lifting them up, inspiring them. It was a perfect lesson for what my journey would become.

3. What's one question you wish you could ask her?

Denise – What she meant about worrying about me because I am most like her. I missed her presence when I took my baby boy home, I would have loved to ask her what to do with him.

Cherie – When you were diagnosed with cancer, how did you feel knowing that you would have to leave your children at such young ages?

Lonnie – How did you manage wearing so many hats (mother, wife, employee, singer)?

4. What type of woman do you think she would be today?

Denise – I think she was evolving in the last three years of her life. I sometimes wonder about that myself. I wonder what type of woman I would be if she were here today.

Cherie – A strong-willed woman of grace; opinionated, yet open to listening to how you feel. Church would still be her everything.

Lonnie – She would be a gospel icon like Albertina Walker, or Cassietta George. Seeing her in front of crowds singing and her response to them always left me in awe. I wonder how I would be different had she lived. The catalyst for my life's work started because it was my way of keeping her name alive.

Mama's legacy lives through each of us. I wonder if we turned out the way she'd hoped, living the lives that she'd envisioned for us? My imagination says that she would say, no, we are doing better than she'd imagined. She will forever be the wind beneath our wings.

I IMAGINE...

As the oldest daughter of an oldest daughter (Mama) of an oldest daughter (her mom) I am full of gratitude and an understanding that family is everything. I am still full of questions and imagination about Mama. As I watch other women with their moms, I ponder what it would it be like to have lunch with my Mama, to travel, or hang out with her. How would we, two adult women, feel about each other? My imagination tells me that we would adore and respect each other's uniqueness.

It's been half a century since Mama was here. The world is so different. I am different. She would be different. I imagine that like me, she would have grown and become a more expansive and even better version of herself. No longer would her answer be "because I said so." Or would it?

Co-author Lonnetta Albright's mother, Augusta Dooley Hunter

"She prayed about everything, and she believed every prayer would be answered. Each of us saw the evidence of what praying to an All-Powerful God could produce."

Strength, Dignity, Wisdom, Faithful, Persevering, Brave and Loving – That's Mom

Written In Honor and Loving Memory of: Mrs. Mabel Adams
AUTHOR: REV. MATILDA ADAMS

> [25] *She is clothed with strength and dignity;*
> *she can laugh at the days to come.*
> [26] *She speaks with wisdom,*
> *and faithful instruction is on her tongue.*
> [27] *She watches over the affairs of her household*
> *and does not eat the bread of idleness.*
> [28] *Her children arise and call her blessed;(NIV)*
> — Proverbs 31:25-28(a)

My Mother was brave. I realize that now. It is her bravery that I choose to share with other women. Although she is no longer with me, each time I share her bravery, it is a way for me to thank her for who she was. Through my gratitude and because of her bravery, I am brave. I am standing on strong shoulders as I tell my story through hers. My hope is in doing so, I will break out of my hiding place in the world. Telling our story is an outlet for me to bravely break free.

It was a humid dry January afternoon in 1980 when the car pulled up. It was my dad's car, but someone else was driving him. He left home a strong, tall, handsome, beloved husband in the prime of his life. He came home, his body paralyzed by a stroke. Now, my mom was faced with taking care of him. Fear attempted to take hold of her but NO – she did not allow it! She made my father comfortable in bed and grabbed her Bible. She took The Word and went to her Father God in prayer. Oh, she knew the stroke, nor the paralysis had taken God by surprise. Still, she needed her marching orders for such a critical assignment. She went into her closet to engage with heaven and came out with a promise. That promise is recorded in Isaiah 54:5 "For thy Maker is thine husband; the Lord of hosts is his name; and thy Redeemer the Holy One of Israel; The God of the whole earth shall he be called." The Lord promised to be her husband. Those words were her foundation as she cared for not only her five children, but her paralyzed husband for the next five years. Her courage in the face of adversity was undeniable. She lived her mantra: her weakness would be made perfect in God's strength.

STRENGTH IN THE FACE OF ADVERSITY!

Mom had a choice. Be afraid and succumb to her fears; or stand in faith believing the God who promised to be "thine husband". Both my parents were teachers. My father had been promoted to the position of Assistant Director of Ghana Education Services when he fell ill. My mom continued to teach and support the leadership team in the local school, where she worked for as an assistant headmistress. We were an average middle-class family. That level of life changed in an instant. She knew what the lifestyle changes would mean, but my mother did not let her children experience fear, not for one minute. She did all she could, including trying to hire the best care professionals money could buy to assist in Dad's care. Although her efforts were futile, she pressed on, never allowing us to see her brokenness. She prayed diligently. It was during these years that my faith in God was shaped. Through our most trying days, my mother would show such strength and undeniable faith.

My mom's walk of faith was not fueled by praying in a heavenly language or stirring worship songs. She knew how to pray in English and her native tongue which was Twi. When she went down on her knees, she prayed in her love language to The Father and that love language always brought results. One morning during the season of my father's disability, she gathered all her children to pray and have our quiet time, as we did regularly. On this morning, she broke down, not out of fear or doubt, but in faith. She shared with us that we only had two Ghana cedis left, which was less than one dollar to feed us. She pulled out the two cedi note, lay it in the middle of the table and proceeded to pray. I distinctly recall how she reminded God that He promised to be her husband. Here she was presenting the children He blessed her with, and her need to feed us before God; confident He would come through.

She prayed with such faith and certainly, then continued with our Bible reading. As she was reading the sacred text for the day, a car pulled into our driveway. We would learn that the answer to her prayer was manifesting quickly. God sent an angel in the form of a friend (who happened to be in the neighborhood) to bring a gift of money. He did it because his friend (my dad) could no longer function as the breadwinner for his family! I hold the lesson of that earnest faith-filled prayer dear to my heart, still. Her faith in God was undeniable and persevering! I understood and witnessed it so often. Seeing the evidence of such great faith changed my life forever. Hallelujah! She prayed about everything, and she believed every prayer would be answered. Each of us saw the evidence of what praying to an All-Powerful God could produce.

PERSEVERANCE OUT OF BROKENNESS

Her persevering spirit brought us through! It was not until I became an adult that I understood the sacrifices my mother made for her children. You see she was born out of wedlock to a teenage mother and endured great challenges growing up. Her birth mother suffered a nervous breakdown after her birth, and she was adopted by her aunt, who loved her so much. For the first 13 years of her life, she lived without a father figure. Her natural father, through divine ordinance, found her and wanted to correct his absence in her life. He was married and decided that my mother should become part of his new family. He took my mother from the village where she was raised to the city to live with him and his wife. While she had hoped the move was a blessing, it turned out to be an exceedingly difficult life. Her stepmother treated her very harshly. The harsh, painful, and unkind treatment from her stepmother became the impetus for her mission to selflessly love her children, no matter what. She was broken; but out of her brokenness came a persevering spirit. No was not an option for her. She had to persevere with dignity! Living with a stepmother who saw her existence as a threat made life more challenging than she could imagine, but she was determined to rise above it all. My mother always instilled the importance of not allowing situations to steal your heart in her children. Proverbs 4:23 supports that lesson, "Keep thy heart with all diligence; for out of it *are* the issues of life." Through all the rejection, disappointment and pain, her faith in God was her shield. She understood and trusted the love of The Father.

GIVING AND RECEIVING LOVE

Mom excelled in school and was enrolled in a teacher's training college. The heart of a teacher is what kept her balanced. She found joy in loving children and the pure loved returned from them brought her great comfort. Her aunt, who became her mother, had an incredible influence on her. This aunt never had children of her own, so my mother was her pride and joy. She shielded her and pushed her to be the best self she could be. Then the disappointment came! Pregnant. No husband. A teenager. Brokenness multiplied, but she knew she had to persevere in prayer and faith. Because she did, the God of wonder showed up. She met my dad while still nursing my older brother. Their love and subsequent marriage became the best thing that could have happened to her. She loved him and her children deeply. Her unwavering love for her children was undeniable. Mom was so stoic, however, that it made it difficult to tell when her world was falling apart. She loved deeply even when she would correct us, even without using the rod. I cannot remember any moment in my life when mother had to discipline me or my siblings with a cane (as was customary when I was growing up). It never happened. She would have stern talks with us and bring The Word of God into the situation.

THE GREATEST DEMONSTRATION OF A MOTHER'S LOVE

In the middle of dealing with a bedridden husband, I fell prey to our generational curse. We lived in a small college town where there were unwritten competitive rules among parents. Every parent wanted their children to excel, so teenage pregnancy was judged harshly. There were no breaks or understanding when children failed. But there I was, a teenager and pregnant; while money was tight, and Dad was still recovering. I thought I would experience her wrath and shame; instead, I was met with love and compassion.

I remember the conversation that fateful day, "I know what must have happened, but I am going to take you and put you back into my womb." What she meant was she was going to cover me so that the world wouldn't see my shame and judge me. She prayed that God would make a way for me to have the baby and finish my education. The news of my pregnancy would disappoint my father terribly, so we chose not to tell him. She covered me at all points. She said my baby was a blessing. I was broken and full of sorrow, but her love and prayers pulled me through. She would not let me sink into despair. I gleaned from her strength and encouragement! So as the Lord would have it, my uncle took me to his home, where I lived with him and his wife (a midwife) until my child's birth.

My mother's love for me was overwhelming. I want mothers to be able to love their children without reservation; and embrace them and their mistakes knowing there is purpose in all things. I want mothers to learn how to pray for their children even if they bring embarrassment. Pray for them through difficult challenges because there is nothing like a mother's love to draw a child out of a difficult place and launch them into their purpose.

Her love for me as a child who supposedly brought her shame by being a teenage mother gave me life. I was never able to have any more children of my own. My daughter is an amazing blessing. My mother could have forced me to have an abortion to save face and get me back on track with school, but that was not an option for her. She believed that since God allowed it, there was greater purpose, so she stood with me in my shame and loved me deeply.

During the first year of college, it was tradition that the new freshman enjoyed a long summer vacation in England. But with Dad's illness presenting hardship, my mother really couldn't give me all the nice things I wanted. During my college summer vacation in 1985, I asked if I could still go to England, but to work to help fund my education. She told me she didn't have the money to buy a ticket; but she would believe God with me. A week later she woke me up early in the morning. She said she heard the Lord say good was going to happen. She believed that God had a plan to get me to England. She determined to see the hand of God move.

With that determination driving, she asked a family friend for a loan to buy me a ticket. Little did she know that God was ordering our steps. I ended up undergoing a life-saving surgical procedure while in England. A large ovarian cyst ruptured and the fluid from the cyst had infected my blood. That emergency surgery would not have been possible if I were at home in Ghana. My mother's choice and sacrifice of her dignity to ask for that loan got me to England,

and saved my life. The memories are too many to share, my heart is filled with warmth and love as I write this to honor my mother. I wish I had one more hour with her on Earth to tell her how grateful I am and to say, thank you. To tell her I know she never had to do anything, but she did everything for her family.

So dear Mama, my angel, my intercessor, my confidante, my friend, thank you. You were an amazing mother to me! I hope I am half the mother you were, Mama even on your last day, your concern for me led you to make sure I had moved into my new office. I am eternally grateful. You are sorely missed; but I am holding my own, keeping my knees to the ground in prayer, loving unconditionally and being brave in all circumstances, knowing that He who has begun a good work in me will bring me to an expected end. I love you Mama.

Co-author Matilda Adams' mother, Mrs. Mabel Adams

"Changing the position of the spotlight changed my heart, allowed me to forgive, and it was then that I understood the profound power of her two words, I tried.

From Anger to Compassion

Written in Honor and Loving Memory of: Paula "Skeet" Bynum
AUTHOR: DR. MICHELLE MCCORMICK

"One of the most important relationships we have is the
relationship we have with our mother."
— Iyanla Vanzant, Author, Television Personality, Life Coach.

Ms. Vanzant's words rang like an alarm in my soul; although I was not able to grasp the full weight of them until my mother passed in 2020. No one provides a manual on how to be the perfect mother or daughter. The best place to find such wisdom and understanding is the Bible. Mothers are given the amazing task of nurturing their daughters so that they in turn are properly equipped to nourish their own children, or others. Mothers do their best with what they have and what they know. Daughters are nourished with whatever the mother has been nourished with. If nourished with rejection, disappointment, and abuse, a mother will pass on the ills that she possesses. If the mother does not heal from her generational hurts, pains, and rejections they tend – sadly - to get passed down to the daughter.

WISDOM IS THE PRINCIPAL THING

Telling my mother's story will help those daughters who have housed anger toward their mothers to turn that anger into compassion.

That transition for me occurred when I took the time to hear and understand my mother's story. Proverbs 4:7 states, "Wisdom is the principal thing; therefore, get wisdom; and with all thy getting, get understanding." That was it! I needed understanding. I could understand her pain and the decisions she made once I understood her story. Understanding her story could empower me to destroy generational curses in my life. Understanding her story was necessary so that I could open the door for forgiveness to enter my heart. I have a clear revelation of several things now. Things that were not evident when my mother was alive. My mother was rejected but full of love. She was damaged, but she tried. She was broken, but fearless.

LOVE THROUGH THE EYES OF REJECTION

The story of my mother's rejection began in the womb. She was given to her aunt at birth. Though there were reasons for it, it created a deep pain which she carried all her life. Grandma Eva, the aunt who raised my mother, was the greatest person I knew. I viewed her through eyes that had seen no wrong. I saw her as a strong and brave woman; traits I would see in my mother later in life. While I am sure that my mother loved Grandma Eva, rejection was evident even in that relationship. My mother would tell me stories of beatings she endured by Grandma Eva's hands. Beatings which would be considered child abuse today. Rejection was the major cause of my mother's brokenness, but my mother was full of love.

My mom had a deep love for family. Family was everything to her. She wanted to love, and she wanted to give love even though at times, I believe she did not know what love looked like. My mother was not taught how to hug, nor did she hear the words "I love you" consistently. That emptiness drove her to give love endlessly. Her deep love was evident in how she showed up for her grandchildren. She would come to their rescue at any time, doing so without hesitation. Her love trickled down to her great-grandchildren, who she would excitedly and willingly babysit, although she was in failing health. I often wondered how someone so full of pain, raised in a lack of love, could be so full of what she lacked. I believe her desire to love through all the rejection and pain was a part of God's heart that He gave to her. Mom had a special grace to love beyond the rejection.

FRAGMENTED PIECES OF LIFE

Whenever you find rejection, being damaged is close behind. Damaged and fragmented tragically describe the soul of my mother. My mother's soul, the source of her emotions and will, was damaged from the rejection of her biological mother. Damaged by the mistreatment of the mother who raised her. Damaged by the man who abused her. Damaged by the children who would not accept her. When I ponder fragments, I am drawn to the times that Jesus would feed the people from fragments of food. We find varying versions of gathered fragments feeding the masses in multiple scriptures (Matthew 14:20; 15:37; Mark 6:43; 8:8; 8:19-20; Luke 9:17). John 6:12, however, presents us with a great understanding about how Jesus felt about fragmented pieces. He instructed the disciples to "gather up the fragments that remain, that nothing be lost." If my mother could have accepted that all her broken, damaged, and fragmented pieces were important to God it would have eased her pain. If she had known that He wanted her to gather the rejection, the pain, the abuse, the frustrations, and the disappointments and present them to Him, she would have known she was wanted. My mother loved God, but she was never able to find her freedom in Him. Her freedom was lost in rejection and the inability to be able to gather her fragmented pieces and brokenness and allow her God to make her whole.

I TRIED

The beginning of understanding my mom's story came during an unfortunate outburst. Angry, hurt, and confused, I lashed out at her verbally. I remember January 4, 2000, as if it were yesterday. That outburst embarrassingly took place in front of my best friends. It is the tears that streamed down my mom's face and the painful regret in her eyes that I remember most. Through her pain, she spoke two words that shifted my anger to compassion. "I tried." Those two words captured me. I was no longer concerned about myself; I needed to understand the story behind the words – "I tried". I realized that my mother was bound by brokenness just like I was.

FEARLESSNESS OVERPOWERED BY BROKENNESS

LaVader, my mom's lifelong friend, described my mother as fearless. I'd asked her for three words to describe my mother who I was seeking to understand anew. She thought the way my mother would move to new cities, where she had no family or friends, represented her fearlessness. In meditating on the countless fearless decisions that my mother made, I became suddenly aware that you can be afraid in some areas and be fearless in others. My mother was afraid to step into her destiny, but she was fearless when it came to traveling and moving to places that she had never been.

Her moving adventures are how we ended up in Providence, Rhode Island when I was 12. I hated that my mother uprooted us from North Carolina. We did not know anyone in Rhode Island, had no knowledge of this place, other than it being one of the states within the United States, and we had no idea why we were going there. I learned the move was done from her place of brokenness and her fearlessness wrapped up in one. Why was it from a place of brokenness? She was following a man who abused her for years. That brutal abuse included her being tied to the bed at times and beat with fish poles, belts, and broomsticks. Once he drove her to a lake at gunpoint and told her to jump. How could these things take place and not affect her children? My siblings and I were damaged mentally, physically, and emotionally by these traumatic experiences. The abusive experiences and her inability (even desire) to get away from them affected our relationships with our mother, each other, and our children. With all the traumatic experiences pressing her down, her brokenness eventually overpowered her fearlessness.

THE FREEDOM TO CHOOSE

My mother's fearlessness became obvious when she made a crucial decision about kidney dialysis treatments. The frustration and the disappointment of being denied placement on the kidney transplant list was a major heartbreak for her. My family nor myself thought that the denial would spark a decision that would change our lives forever. On April 7, 2020, while sitting at my desk, my mother called me to tell me that she had decided to stop the dialysis treatments she had been undergoing for 13 years. Because the dialysis treatments were keeping my mother alive, I knew the dire consequences of her decision. The only thing that could change it was God performing a miracle. I can recall the exact words I said to her upon hearing her decision. I sensed she needed to hear them, "Mom, I have watched you all your life make decisions for everyone else; this time make the decision for you." Twelve days after that decision, the woman I called Mother, the woman who was rejected but full of love, damaged but tried to be the best mother she could, and the woman that was broken but fearless left this life the way she chose to. She did not get to choose how she entered this life; she had no voice in choosing who would raise her, but her fearlessness gave her the freedom to choose how she departed this life.

Paula, affectionately known as Skeet, is the woman that I called mom. For almost 49 years God allowed her to share a space with me.

My own brokenness stole the opportunity for me to realize how this amazing woman was the person I had become. Rejection did not rob her of the desire to give love. I could not see the multiple ways she loved because I was blinded by my own pain.

She was damaged mentally, emotionally, and physically by the years of abuse that I watched her endure; but she tried! My mother tried with the skills and tools that she had. She did not do everything right, but she did not do everything wrong either. I had to offer her the same grace that I did not realize I would need from my own children when I echoed her words "I tried."

At the age of 37, my mom was diagnosed with breast cancer and the prescribed treatments created problems in her kidneys. Through every season of her life, though she was broken, she was a fearless woman. It took fearlessness to make some of the selfless decisions she made for her children. The day that I looked in my mother's eyes and saw the pain deeply rooted in her soul, was the day that I understood the meaning of selfless love. Selfless love allowed me to take my story out of the spotlight and put my mother's story there. Changing the position of the spotlight changed my heart, allowed me to forgive, and it was then that I understood the profound power of her two words "I tried."

Co-author Dr. Michelle McCormick's mother, Paula "Skeet" Bynum

"Even though my mother is no longer with me, she lives in my heart, mind, and spirit. Her impartations have been the breadcrumbs left behind that have gotten me through life's most challenging moments."

Selfless Sacrifice

Written in Honor and Loving Memory of: Kate Stephen
AUTHOR: RHONDA ETHERIDGE

"Story is our escort; without it we are blind. Does a blind man own his escort? No, neither do we the story; rather it is our story that owns us and directs us."
— Chinua Achebe, Author, Anthills of the Savannah

WISDOM, EMPATHY AND COMPASSION

The school's receptionist didn't believe that the olive-complexion woman with dense black hair, thin black eyebrows and coal-black eyes standing in front of her was the mother of the lighter-skinned girl the woman wanted to remove from school that day. The receptionist began pulling my records to verify that she was my parent and had permission to pick me up. When the secretary came to retrieve me from the classroom, she whispered something to my teacher, and I remember the perplexed look on my teacher's face. My mom was standing outside the front office and as we approached, the secretary looked at her and stated, "Here she is. Can't be safe enough these days."

As my classmates transitioned to class, I could hear them whispering, "She got a white mom." "Ooh, her mom's white." At that moment, I resented her for coming to my school and embarrassing me in front of my classmates. Didn't she know how hard I had worked to make myself invisible among my peers? When I started elementary school, I was ridiculed and called names such as red-bone, yellow-bone, yellow-hammer, and white girl to mock my light-skinned complexion, but the teasing and name-calling had stopped, and I didn't want to be teased again. When I came to school the next day, my classmates began questioning if my mother was white. I denied the woman who picked me up from school was my mom. I claimed, "The lady who picked me up was my mom's friend. That wasn't my mom." I felt bad for denying my mother. The woman who gave birth to, loved, and nurtured me was denied because I selfishly wanted to be accepted by my peers. Undeniably, I felt ashamed of what I had done. It was wrong, but this was my first experience with colorism in the Black community. By the end of the school day, I had convinced myself that my actions were warranted because I had to protect my mom. Imagine that: I had to tell a lie to protect my mom from the evil whispers of first and second graders. Reflecting on this incident, I am drawn to Proverbs 16:18 that warns, "Pride goes before destruction, a haughty spirit before a fall." Interestingly, my mother would often recite this passage, especially if someone were thinking too highly of themselves or contemplating doing something for the wrong reason.

Author William Hurt said it best in the short story *Scarlet Ibis* when the narrator speaks of having "a knot of cruelty borne by the stream of love." The narrator taught his handicapped brother to walk, which is an impressive feat; however, he does so to spare himself the embarrassment of having a brother who could not walk. As humans, we sometimes do wonderful things for the wrong reason. Denying my mother that day was definitely one of the times I allowed my desire to fit in and be accepted by my classmates get the best of me. It wasn't because she needed physical protection from a group of young children. It was because I was disheartened by my classmates' reactions toward her. They couldn't see past her skin color and embrace the wonderful mother she was, so I felt compelled to shelter my mother from my classmates' taunts.

If you want to know who you are or why you are prone to do the things you do in life, the answer to that question can be found in the stories of one's mother. Mothers define who and what we are as well as how we show up in the world more than anyone else. Religious and civil rights activist, Malcolm X said it best, "The mother is the first teacher of the child. The message she gives to that child, that child gives to the world." Mothers are givers of life. Through God's divine design, mothers carry humanity.

MOTHERS ARE THE INTERCONNECTION TO OUR PAST AND OUR FUTURE.

My mother, Kate Stephen, poured into her children all that she had while living in a society that did not respect or acknowledge her as an equal human being. Growing up in Texas was not a desirable or ideal environment during an era in which our country's history had created communities full of discrimination, racism, sexism, and a climate of political extremism. It was even more challenging for women, especially women of color. She viewed her children as gifts the world had given her; and what became her purpose in life was safeguarding them from the harsh past while preparing them for the future.

My mother's stories, shared with me, helped shape my life and mold the moral values I hope to pass on to my children. When I feel like nothing is going right, and I have lost my path, memories of my mother guide and help me to keep moving forward. My mom desired more than anything to be a mother but had difficulty conceiving. My aunts often spoke of how my mom loved children and how she helped take care of her younger siblings growing up. She was also a second mother to three of my aunt's older children prior to having her own. After years of hormone fertility treatments, my mom gave birth to her first child at the age of thirty and was ecstatically happy. Two months after birth, the baby died of sudden infant death syndrome (SIDS) and my mother was devastated. The death of a child is one of the most painful events that can happen to a mother. My mom experienced an intense emotional crisis of grief, guilt, and anger. The dreams she had of watching her child grow were gone and so much of what she wanted and planned for was lost. Many family members and friends spoke of how my mom was to them, a condensed narration of a living Bible.

A WALKING, LIVING BIBLE

I admired my mother's honesty, willingness to listen and her ability to conceptualize life's tenets. She knew the Bible like the back of her hand and would use the stories and scriptures as a compass to help individuals through life's trials and tribulations without being preachy or judgmental. It didn't matter what was going on in her life, she would stop everything for the opportunity to bring clarity to one's thoughts and ideas. If someone was going through something, she was always a secure ear. My mother's humility, love and compassion for people left an indelible impression on my life.

Our house was a sanctuary for individuals looking for peace of mind and spirit. Our home would randomly and often be filled with those who my mother lovingly referred to as "shut-outs." Shut-outs were individuals who were called crazy or good-for-nothing, by others in the neighborhood. To my mother, they were God's children in search of life's answers. They would spend hours in our home talking to my mother as my sister and I would hide and eavesdrop. We discovered the depth of our mother's selfless acts of listening, sharing, and giving during those times. Often, she would give people money to make ends meet even though our family struggled financially. She would always say, "When you give to others, give in love and don't expect to get it back. If you do get it back, consider it a gift of God's love."

She gave unconditionally to her family, loved ones and friends, and I respected that. I have her uncanny desire to mentor and help others in their personal and professional growth. As a professional educator, I am in my element when I'm adding value to others through listening, answering questions, providing knowledge and encouragement. Teaching inspires individuals to transcend beyond their own capabilities and become a source of inspiration for others. It is the gift that keeps on giving and one that my mom passed on to me.

SILENT SACRIFICE GAVE VOICE TO THE VOICELESS

My mother gave me my voice and willingness to speak up in uncomfortable situations as well as the fearless gift to ask questions. She encouraged me to be respectful and courteous in pursuit of insight and truth, which I surmise is a direct result of what she had endured in her life. As a 19-year-old woman full of hope and dreams, my mother began her path to womanhood - voiceless; she was blindsided by my father's request for her hand in marriage. Instead of discussing it with my mother and asking her to marry him, my father chose to go to her father and discuss marrying my mother with him first. My grandfather gave his consent. Not to disrespect her father or bring shame upon her family, my mother agreed to marry my father. As my mother gave her summation of the facts, she shared, "The men in those days made the decision for the family. It was the way it was back then. The Bible says, "Honor thy father and thy mother: that thy days may be long upon the land."

As a teenager having this conversation with my mother, whom I revered as the smartest, fiercest woman I knew, I couldn't fathom why she agreed to marry a man she initially was not ready to commit her life to and begin raising a family. It wasn't until later in life I came to cherish and respect the reason my mom married my father and the significance of the words, "Thy will be done". I never understood the comprehensive meaning of those words my mom would recite when she didn't know what to expect or what specific outcome she would have to endure. Years later, she shared the meaning of those words with me as they pertained to her life. "Yes, I loved your father; however, I wanted to wait and get married later in my life. I had dreams that I wanted to accomplish. But sometimes in life, we make our plans and God laughs." She explained that God has the final say, and it is His will that guides us. It is not our will to be done, but God's. My mom's commitment to my father and to our family was in direct correlation to her commitment to God and His will.

This defining moment gave me deeper insight into how courageous and selfless my mother was in pursuing the life God had commanded for her. Although the initial dreams my mother had for her life were no more, God blessed her with the courage to dream and achieve many others. My mother and father were married for fifty-six years, owned their home, raised four children and were grandparents to five children. Although my mother was not able to go to college after high school, she earned a Certificate in Biblical Studies and applied her knowledge and skills to help others facing challenges. In life, we will have disappointments, and we will get knocked down, but we must be courageous in finding the new things God has in store for us.

As an adult, I had a heartfelt conversation with my mom about my behavior and what I'd done that day in elementary school. I am grateful I had that opportunity. It gave me a sense of reprieve and I took great solace in her response, "That's okay. It's not the first time I've been denied." Although honest, it was also profoundly unfortunate. Her words illuminating her endurance through a dark and shameful chapter of our country's past, and the pain of living in a world of inequality, full of rejection, denial, and involuntary sacrifice where women were to be seen and not heard.

Stories about my mother allow me to pause, read life's road signs again, reorient myself and get back on track. Even though my mother is no longer with me, she lives in my heart, mind, and spirit. Her impartations have been the breadcrumbs left behind that have gotten me through life's most challenging moments. Although tattered and worn, my mother was able to move from a life of pain and heartache into a life of opportunity for her children.

Co- author Rhonda Etheridge's mother, Kate Stephen

"She (or Mama) was our rock, our counsel, our greatest fan, and our best friend. Most importantly she kept us safe."

It's Just for a While

Written in Honor and Loving Memory of: Ella Jewell Dooley Senior
AUTHOR: SIR STANLEY SENIOR

The great crooner Frank Sinatra had a song called "My Way". Some of the lyrics Sinatra sang says, "I've loved, I've laughed and cried, I've had my fill of losing. Yes, there were times, I'm sure you knew when I bit off more than I can chew. But through it all when there was doubt, I ate it up and spit it out. I faced it all, and I stood tall and did it my way." My mama certainly can make that claim. Doing it her way led to an amazing life.

Mama is one of the most powerful words, describing one of the most impactful people. In China, she is called Mu-ching. In Japanese, she is Haha. In India, she is Mahgee or Ma. No matter the language, Mother or Mama, invokes engaging, exciting, and influential memories and emotions. A friend and I chatted about the thing we most admired in each other. Resiliency was the quality they admired about me. That is a quality I learned from my mother. Mama was the most resilient (among other adjectives) human being I knew.

Ella Jewell Dooley Senior was born March 3, 1936, in Damascus, Arkansas; one of 11 children. She was married at 19 and had two children before moving from that small town to Los Angeles, California in 1960.

The move to Los Angeles came with issues in the marriage. Shortly after experiencing the move and the marital challenges, I was born in May 1961. Her marriage ended soon after, so she packed up her children, moved out and never looked back. Years later she revealed that she had no plan at the time, but she developed one quickly. That plan: pursue her dreams, set goals toward that, and drag (as she would say) us along with her. It was a great ride. She pursued a nursing career while my siblings were in school, and I was with a babysitter. While in training, she would work a split shift as a customer service representative for a telephone company. This afforded her the time to get my siblings to school and be able to pick us all up later in the day. Her zest for being a people person increased her knack for success. Leaving nursing, and customer service, she would dive into the airline industry. She became the first Black female reservation agent, for Western Airlines, a popular carrier at the time. Always one to keep more than one income stream fluid, before it became a standard financial practice, Mom also modeled. That modeling opened the door to her appearance on the previously popular game show "What's My Line"

As her careers shifted, so did where we called home. Every three years, we had a new home in a different Los Angeles area; though she made sure we landed in better than average areas. Somehow, between careers and frequent moves, she was able to keep us in school and maintain our medical and dental care. That was a major feat in the 1960s and 70s when healthcare wasn't a priority.

Mom's style, demeanor and sense of class made our friends think we were rich. We were the only kids I knew whose mom had a tailor make their clothes. I hated that because I was always overdressed among my peers. She didn't care, it was important to her that we looked good.

Moving into the 1970s, she decided to make a bold and risky career move. She decided to work for herself. She secured a license to sell life insurance and dove headfirst into an industry dominated by White males. During that era, it was highly unusual for a woman, White or Black, to succeed in that industry. She went on to work for

Prudential Insurance and became a multi-million dollar producing agent/producer. Plaques heralding her success proudly hung on display in our home and her office.

Mom would throw her all into her work; whatever the work was at any given time. Amidst that, she made sure we lived a full life. A bit of a socialite, she learned the art of holding her own in any environment and was quite respected because of it. As a kid, I had the privilege of going with her on appointments or sitting with her at her office. I would marvel at her ability to multitask (something I think I might have picked up from her).

She was always big on family, and maintained close ties with ours, no matter where life took us. She became the anchor to every family member who visited us in L.A., needing a place to land. Because family was important to her, we celebrated all the holidays, and other special gatherings at our house. Mama also played the roles of father figure, Santa Claus, Easter bunny, the Thanksgiving chef, and the tooth fairy. I believed in them all until I didn't. My brother Cordell would add that she was our rock, our counsel, our greatest fan, and our best friend. Most importantly she kept us safe.

Mama was also a great cook and would often spoil us with chef quality dishes. I fondly remember the days when those tantalizing dishes would bring folks to the house to play cards and dominoes and listen to the Motown sound, the Philly sound and her favorites, Ella Fitzgerald, Aretha Franklin, and Dionne Warwick. There would be a lot of loud talking, but my mom's voice could be heard over all of them. She had the greatest laugh. In it, you heard how much she enjoyed life.

My mama always had the right words to say even when she didn't, and she was frustratingly intuitive. She knew where you were going in conversation without asking. She could finish your sentences. Her personality was electrifying and positive. Her spiritual faith, which she gained from her parents, was always evident. She stood strong in that faith foundation and certainly, it played a significant part of her continual and repeated success. She was a true child of God, loving and self-sacrificing, always there to give of herself to anyone in need.

During the '70s she was busy and always on the scene in Los Angeles. So, she had brushes with influential people because of her work and prominence. She worked on Tom Bradley's mayoral campaign. She would socialize with entertainers like R & B singer Bobby Womack, jazz vocalist Dee Dee Bridgewater and professional football legend Deacon Jones. She once told me a story about meeting the phenomenal jazz and blues singer, Nancy Wilson. Nancy was excited to meet her because everybody said that they strikingly favored each other. She also met singer Mavis Staples of the R & B group The Staples Singers. Ms. Staples adopted me as a godson after seeing me with my mom. She thought I was cute. Mom also told me stories of real estate deals with a guy named Donald Trump. At the time, those in the industry referred to him as a slumlord. Mom moved on from selling insurance, landing in the financial services industry with Investors Diversified Services.

After I graduated from high school in 1979, in Santa Monica, she made a "no kids" move to Denver, Colorado. For the first time in her life, she was on her own. She reinvented herself and worked for Hertz Rent-A-Car driving buses at the airport. After 10 great years in Colorado, she moved to Houston then back to Los Angeles, specifically to the Rancho Cucamonga / Ontario area. Never wanting to be without a job she went to work for a window blind company. From there, she took on to her last job as an office manager for a Miracle-Ear franchise in Rancho Cucamonga that ended in 2012.

Now in her seventies, capitalizing on her corporate and customer service acumen, she started a new business called JDS Enterprises. The company contracts medical billing and coding services. She took on the business after earning certification in the field. Mama had an unshakable strength to just keep going, and to live in the present moment. If she was suffering from any of life's problems, she did not show it. She kept moving forward with a positive attitude. She later told me that, no matter what she did, she never had a concrete plan. She would simply allow life to take her where it would. She has no regrets for choosing that route. An independent woman, who refused to live in the past, she never remarried. She relished and celebrated her life as an independent woman. Mama passed away October 10, 2020, at 84 years of age. Although health issues became insurmountable, she was still pursuing life and living it as fully as she could. Her body couldn't keep up with her mind's possibilities. She was still independent and living in her own home, which was always comfortable, organized, and peaceful. My sister Sharon would say in her eulogy that, "Mama chose achievement and success. You had to be careful where you walked when near her because there was always glass covering the floor as she shattered those instituted glass ceilings"

There's not a day that goes by that I don't think about my mother. When she was with us, I was always thinking about her and her well-being. My mother was one of the greatest women ever. There's no bigger figure in my life. I'm one of the luckiest human beings to have been raised by such a great woman. The things I accomplished are nothing compared to what she was all about. Every part of my life is about her. I, and my siblings, are just an extension of everything that she was.

I end my celebration of Mama, with a short poem that she penned:

"It's Just for a While"

I want to live, just for a while.
We are given just a while.
Not long, not short, just a while.
I want to live, live –
Live full of joy, just for a while.
Having faith, trusting powerfully
and loving all,
just for a while.

Love each day with fullness,
walk through each day by His grace.
Give thanks all day,
know His goodness by faith
and live in all His glory, full of joy.
Just for a while.
Not long, not short, just a while.
I'll slow down,
I won't despair,
remember to smile,
remember this is just for a while.
Life gets tough,
becomes a trial,
but smile,
remember –
It's just for a while.
Life is good,
feeling at the top of the pile.
Don't stop —
remember it's just for a while.

Co-author Sir Stanley Seniors' mother, Ella Jewell Dooley Senior

"No one ever wakes up asking to have a disorder of any kind. You do not ask for it, and you pray that you will be healed from it. You do not want to be treated differently, less than, and unusual. You do not want to be seen as incapable. You want people to see you as a normal person, to hear your voice concerning your needs, and to be treated fairly."

Embracing Her Legacy

Written in Honor of: Sadie Delphenia Wilkins
AUTHOR: TRINA WILKINS

*"The most authentic thing about us is our capacity to
create, to overcome, to endure, to transform, to love and to
be greater than our suffering."*
— Ben Okri Nigerian Poet/Novelist

THE ROAD OF LIFE

Life is a very mystical journey as it cannot be predicted ahead of
time. No one has access to the future to know how to navigate
the twists, turns, or ups and downs of life. Life can be the greatest
adventure or the darkest road to travel. During the journey there may
be times that you feel alone, but you never are. The Bible reminds us
in Deuteronomy 31:8 (NIV); "The Lord himself goes before you and
will be with you; he will never leave you nor forsake you. Do not be
afraid; do not be dismayed."

I have witnessed the hand of God orchestrating the people that
He has allowed to cross my path. This has been true in friendships,
romantic and professional relationships, and in my family. Some
have been here for a season, while others are lifetime covenants. I
have encountered many amazing, unique, and creative people. I have
had the opportunity to meet phenomenal Black women with varying

roles in my life from teacher, counselor, coach, to spiritual leader. Although I have been blessed to encounter so many phenomenal women, by far the greatest woman in my life has been my mother.

AFFECTIONATELY KNOWN AS "SUPERVISOR", I CALL HER MOMMY

Families call the woman of the home many different names. They are known as: Matriarch, Mama, Mother, Madea, Ma, Mum, Maw, Matushka, and Madre. My mother is Sadie Delphenia Wilkins; some call her Del, but I call her Mommy. Although I call her Mommy; in our family, my mother was coined "Supervisor." This name was given to her by a cousin at a family reunion. As the family was helping to decorate the room, my mother was instructing everyone where to put things, how the program should go, and who should do certain parts. My cousin would reply at each command, "Yes, Supervisor." If someone asked my cousin a question, she would point toward my mom and tell them to, "ask the supervisor." Every family gathering since that day, when my mother arrives, everyone greets her with the name that fits her perfectly. Mommy was always overseeing, assisting, and managing the family and our multiple events. This was a natural talent for her. She liked working with computers, organizing, and paying attention to details. During her life she has assisted churches, people in the community, as well as family members on special projects.

SADIE DELPHENIA WILKINS - FIVE FEET THREE BUT SIX FEET TALL!

Sadie was born as the oldest daughter of three children in a small town called Lawrenceville, Virginia. In her youth she helped her family out by working on a farm. She told me she had to work long, hard hours in picking assorted crops, in the sweltering heat. Her hands would hurt from the work. She had to work on the farm because she was the oldest. While she toiled, she would watch her siblings playing and making mud pies. Her family moved north to New Jersey when she was 12 years old. The move was in hopes of better opportunities.

My mother is small in stature, but big in personality. She may only be five feet three inches tall; but her presence towers over six feet! She speaks with intelligence, walks with a dignified strut, and commands respect in any room she enters. She never let the challenges of life stop her from letting her presence be known. She was not known for being weak, or allowing people to walk over, mistreat, or belittle her. No matter who challenged her or what circumstance was in front of her, she was going to stand her ground. Not only were you going to respect her, but you were also going to respect her loved ones.

As a young child, I was bullied in school because I was quiet, or I would not do what other people wanted me to do. I was not a follower, and I reasoned that if I was going to get in trouble, it was not going to be because I did what they wanted me to do. On one occasion, I got into a fight on my way home from school with a classmate. As I was walking home, her friend, a young boy, grabbed my arms restraining me. He held me as she punched me all over my body. I left there with a black eye. When I got home and my mother saw me, she refused to let the incident end the way it did. The next day, my mother drove around with me in the car until she found the girl who gave me the black eye. She told her that she is not to put her hands on me ever again, and if she did, she would come to her house to have a discussion with her and her mother. I never had a problem out of that girl again. In that moment, I learned how important it is to defend yourself even if you lose. I knew that Mother would protect me, keep me safe, and that she is not who you want to mess with.

DEL, THE FASHIONISTA!

Del was always known for wearing stylish clothes. She had a flair for going into any store and putting the most stylish outfit together. She may not have known what the latest trends were, but when she was done shopping, she was trend worthy.

My mother has always had a vibrant spirit. She loves to dance, play games, and has a passion for reading. Once she graduated from high school, the sky was the limit. She found the love of her life, got married, and had her most precious gift in the world; me - her daughter Trina.

THEN EVERYTHING CHANGED

Unfortunately, life was not a fairy tale for my mother. Unforeseen and uncontrollable events took place in her life that would change her destiny. Sadie woke up one morning and the world became dark. Reality became a far distance. All thoughts, places, and people were different. She could not comprehend or understand the changes she was enduring and only knew things were not the same. Suddenly, her life became appointments, tests, overnight stays, and different treatments to manage this new change. There were times that things would be going great; while other moments would be the greatest struggles of her life.

My mother grew up in an era where speaking about having an emotional disorder was taboo. Things of this nature were never allowed to be spoken of and oftentimes hidden from others. She faced many deplorable labels, stigmas, and misguided beliefs. She was shunned, misunderstood, isolated, mocked, disrespected, and made to feel inferior. This experience affected her internally. A woman who was once vibrant, had her light diminished. She believed she was unloved and incapable of thriving in life. She was no longer open to the possibilities of dreams, freedom, and peace. She buried her feelings inside, became distant, cold, and numb.

I remember seeing the changes, challenges, and concerns my

mother went through to survive. I have seen her in tears, trying to find a way to put food on the table. I have seen her between jobs and looking for work. All the while, wrestling with managing a marriage, a home, and a child. I witnessed her being rejected by others, no matter how hard she tried to fit in. I watched her fall to the pressure of not being able to cope with the stress of daily life. I have heard her cry out to God asking Him to please send help.

Although there have been dark moments in her life; I have seen God's light and love shine on her. I have witnessed her overcome things that would have killed others. She has a quiet inner strength and courage that springs forth and moves mountains. The most beautiful thing about watching her life's story is seeing her unchanging hand with God. She may not understand why an emotional disorder invaded her; but she continues to seek God and read the Bible daily. Philippians 4:13, "I can do all things through Christ which strengthens me"; is one of her favorite scriptures. Growing up I would often hear that scripture echoed in our home.

Now in my adult years, I see my mother's persistent struggle to maintain the ability to manage her life. Still fighting for a form of normalcy, she seeks to be independent in every area of her life. Living life on her own terms and making her own decisions is critical to her. Most importantly though, she desires to be loved and accepted for who she is. At her sixtieth birthday party she spoke so profoundly about her life experience. She quipped about how no one ever wakes up asking to have a disorder of any kind.

She said, "You do not ask for it, and you pray that you will be healed from it. You do not want to be treated differently, less than, and unusual. You do not want to be seen as less than or incapable. You want people to see you as a normal person, to hear your voice concerning your needs, and to be treated fairly."

Others know her as wife, daughter, sister, aunt, and cousin. I know her as Mommy. Every now and then, I get to experience the warmth and love from the person not hiding behind the shell, and then I can embrace her. I can receive that hug of assurance that only a mother can give. I am privileged to receive her wisdom. I am blessed to hear her belly laugh when she thinks I say something funny. I get to see her still styling and profiling in her beautifully assembled outfits. I get to watch her as little girls do, and see her dance (oh how she loves to dance and listen to music), put together puzzles, or decorate the house. I get to witness her embracing the sun, sitting on the deck, or listening to the waves at the beach. I rejoice watching her give praise and thanks to the Heavenly Father for blessing her daily.

Today, I honor you, Mommy, for your example of endurance on the earth. I honor you for displaying your continuous spirit to fight and overcome obstacles, and for your courage, strength, and steadfastness in life. I honor your ability to love and guide. I want you to know that you have been heard, you are seen, you are not forgotten, and will always be loved, no matter what life throws at you. I am giving you your flowers now and want you to know that I am proud of you. I am proud of you for not giving up, for finding the good in all circumstances, and continuing to shine bright in a very dark world. I acknowledge that I am thankful, and I am blessed to call you my Mommy! You are a Proverbs 31, phenomenally amazing woman. I am thankful to God for choosing you to be my mother; because you are a splendid example of how to press through trials and live victoriously. I call you blessed and praise you. Mommy you are the strongest woman I know. You are my shero!

Co-author Trina Wilkins' mother, Sadie Delphenia Wilkins

"The strength of a mother is second to none. Even when she is beyond exhausted, both mentally and physically; nothing will stop her from caring for her children. It takes someone really brave to be a mama, someone strong to raise a child, and someone special to love another more than herself."

Indestructible

Written in Honor of: Grace Adwoa Sekyere
AUTHOR: DR. VIDA-LYNN ASARE

"The strength of a mother is second to none. Even when
she is beyond exhausted, both mentally and physically,
nothing will stop her from caring for her children. It
takes someone really brave to be a mama, someone strong
to raise a child, and someone special to love another more
than herself."
— Proud Happymama

My intention for writing this chapter is to give myself an opportunity to explore my relationship with my mother; to step back and examine our relationship, which is one characterized by love, through distance. She is extraordinarily strong, brave, and caring, however through this writing I found it important to explore how her being "all things for all people" also diminished her ability to be always physically present. She was stretched in so many ways.

A WOMAN OF STRENGTH

A member of our family was being abused by her husband. Her husband had strong financial and social statuses in the community, was very influential and popular; so, he felt he was above scrutiny. No one – including professional counselors - could convince him to change.

One day, my mother, a bold advocate, told me she acted in the matter. She said, "I called him and warned him that this would be the last time he would ever abuse, demean or put his wife down again! I quoted the Bible to him!"

Of course, I asked, "Mommy, do you think he will listen this time?"

Mommy said, "Yes! He did not say a word because of how I approached him!"

She was right! That situation was resolved soon after that. Intervening in challenging situations is normal for my mom. She is not afraid to step in and rescue anyone who is being hurt, abused, taken advantage of, or anyone who is unable to defend themselves. She always raises her voice in advocacy for those needing emotional strength and financial support.

PASSION IS HER MIDDLE NAME!

Second Samuel 6:14 which states that "And David danced before the Lord with all his might..."

My mother is so full of energy! She has seasons in her life when her exuberance peaks and when you are around her the room always lights up! You see this magically when she dances, which she does so passionately! At church, she serves as the praise dance minister, and she joyfully moves to the tune of the music surrounded by other wonderful dancers. Her dancing for God is but the tip of the iceberg. She is also known as the "Dance Queen" at our family get togethers!

I recall one of her birthday celebrations; she requested a specific song to dance to. For whatever reason, the wrong song was played, and she refused to take the dance floor. To her, the dance movements had to accompany the chosen song. The meaning of the song was so important and intimate to her that she wanted the audience to feel the full effect of its message through her movements.

For a while, all the visitors sat waiting in expectation to ensure that what she had chosen was indeed played. Then, when she took the dance floor, her movements were passionate, energetic, and fun; the atmosphere was filled with the excitement of what she was able to release! Her passion was on full display.

Her dance was contagious!

Her dance was attractive!

Her dance lightened up the room!

Always! Every single time she took the dance floor!

EVERYDAY EXTRAORDINARY SACRIFICES

Mom's life's goal is to ensure that the neglected are taken care of. Many times, that meant giving her financial support to ensure that families were stabilized, and needy children were fed and clothed. She often took unfortunate children into our home, provided them with whatever they needed - using her own resources. As they grew, she encouraged them to learn a trade or to pursue a degree from a great university. I can personally count more than twenty-five people who have been able to complete their tertiary education because of her unselfish sacrifices. Because of her, many who had no hope, earned degrees, learned skills and are successful. That is the sacrifice of a loyal friend – a true advocate!

This pushing for more in life is a personality trait of my mom that I find so commendable. She has always been keen on succeeding. She is one of those people that knew making it was the only option for her. She doesn't know the word no when it comes to what she is striving for. She would sacrifice time, resources, strength, and everything and everyone else to make sure that a goal you set before you is achieved. My mom did not get the opportunity to go to a higher level of education; so, it was critically important for her that all her children and even children in communities where she lived and served had the opportunity to do so. This passion of hers is one

I am glad to say I inherited. I have always been determined to go as high as I could, and grab hold to the opportunities that come. When it comes to achievement and education, I go for the gusto and Mom is there happily celebrating.

Even in our own family, Mom always makes sure there is food on the table. When she visits her grown children and grandchildren, you can't make her relax. She has to do something! I can remember times when Mommy would cook seven dishes in one day and the following day, she would get up and cook with that same fervency! Mom is as passionate and serious about what she cooks as she is about dancing. Not only must it be delicious, (and it always is), it must be nutritious and well-balanced.

I would ask, "Mom, didn't you cook yesterday? Why do you have to cook again?"

She would always say, "While I am here visiting, I want my children and grandchildren to have good food and dessert after they eat."

As she happily toiled in the kitchen, pouring her love into every dish, she would have ice packs on her back to dull the pain from working so hard the previous day! I would catch her rubbing on pain ointment while preparing to cut onions for another meal! If sacrificing her tired body were not enough, she would sacrifice financially and assure our refrigerators are filled before she leaves. The same sacrificial love and service followed her to each of her ten children's homes.

That is my Mom!

It is hilarious to me as I write this thinking about her and the way she still needs to assure the children are eating. My siblings and I joke about it all the time. Mom doesn't simply come to your house and cooks; she brings LOTS of food with her. She came to our home once from visiting my sister in Ohio; and I met her at the airport. She had drinks and food in her carry-on bag. I reminded her that she didn't need to do things like that. But she insisted that what was in that bag was for her grandchildren and that was the end of that conversation.

If she is visiting and you have laundry that needs to be managed, she's on the job. It's something she doesn't think about. She actually comes in with her own laundry detergents! I think it's hilarious, but it is who Mom is.

By the time mother was 18 she had lost her father, two older siblings, and her younger brother to unrelated incidents. Her younger brother and one older sister died from sickness. Her father died of natural causes. And one older sister died in an accident.

She became a single parent for her ten children and additional adopted ones, yet she was unafraid and bold. Her capacity to flourish under adversity in her early years became a survival technique for her to thrive when confronted with adversity. My mom is not afraid to share her trials and tribulations with our family: her painful divorce, raising ten children, the difficult separation from her children for years at a time. She shares the years she spent working two to three jobs at a time in the United States. She did not attend college, but she walked the campuses of many colleges to support our dreams.

While Mommy was fighting so hard for others, part of me believes there was a time in her life where she wished someone had fought for her. It's difficult to give the details of my mother's very public and extremely bitter divorce. That divorce forced her to move abroad and away from her children for many years. Mom never healed from that season of her life. I believe she sought that healing in a renewed presence in her children and grandchildren's lives. She often expresses that she wishes - even though her children are all adults with families in various places - that we all lived in a single house.

Mom worked as a secretary in Ghana's parliament house. When she met my father at the age of 18, she resigned, and they started a business. Their business expanded into an import and export company. With that, they acquired houses, cars, and social status. My parents were also leaders in the church they attended. My father had an extra-marital affair with one of the women in their church who was a very instrumental women's fellowship leader. My mother endured neglect, as well as emotional and financial abuse, and eventually, she left her marriage. She left the business, houses, and cars behind; not by choice, but because the man owned the assets in the marriage in those days. Legal and social support for women who found themselves in such predicaments were nearly non-existent. She stepped out of her marriage with only her clothes and just enough for transportation away from her home. She lived with family members and depended on them for food and necessities before traveling to the United Kingdom and then the United States.

My mother has never stopped talking about the long hours that she worked, the sleepless nights, and the sacrifices she had to make while she was married to my father. I am not sure whether she felt humiliated or vindicated when the relationship between my father and the woman turned into a public spectacle. She did not go back to entrepreneurship after her divorce, yet she has counseled and supported her children who are called into the field to thrive and flourish.

A FORCE FROM A VERY YOUNG AGE

My mother's name is Grace. She also goes by Mansa, which means she is the third female in a row. She was born in a town called Koforidua in Ghana. She had two older siblings and two younger brothers. At an early age, Mom was given to her aunt, who never had children. In those days people perceived it as an honorable gesture. Mother had difficulties because of not knowing her biological mother and growing up in poor conditions. She was denied food, education, and other basic needs. At the age of seven, she stood up for herself and announced a hunger strike, insisting that her conditions improve. She would not be intimidated and prevented from attending school.

At the age of ten she went to live with her birth parents.

Later, she had to sacrifice her college education to start working so that she could help to pay for her younger brother's education. She grew up in an era of gender stereotyping when girls were less likely than boys to go on to higher education.

This literary honoring of her gives me an opportunity to reflect, heal and to celebrate her. I want daughters of strong mothers with huge global, social assignments to be like me, able to be a child/a woman that understands where these special moms come from divinely and personally. Able to understand the significance of their lives, and able to paint a picture of women who loved, served, cared, and advocated powerfully, often without healing from their own pains, and often feeling forgotten, just like her children.

CARING IS JOB #1

Though my internal struggles with the mother I wanted and the mother who was a champion advocate often clouded my relationship with my mother in my younger years, I was never conflicted about one thing - my mother cared. She cared and she doted on her children. There were times when we had to go to church or attend a special occasion, and Mom always took extra measures to make sure that everyone's clothes were laid out and ironed, sometimes fixing loose buttons, or trimming loose threads. She spent a lot of time fixing our hair. After we had a mouthwatering breakfast (that she prepared), and all the beds were made (by her), it would be time for us to leave. That's when she would realize that while we were all dressed up and looking beautiful, she hadn't even taken her shower!

We always reminded Mom that she could leave us to finish getting ready for ourselves. But she was used to putting everyone first. So often, on so many occasions we would encourage her to think about herself before she thinks about us. But she would always say, "It's my goal to make sure that you are looking beautiful! Doing that makes me happy!"

Mom has evolved so much as she has aged. She has learned to give herself far more self-care. It is wonderfully pleasing to see that. I remember when she would give beyond boundaries. She would be there for anyone without thought, as if it were her responsibility to jump in and provide. I don't know if this is evolving because she is aging, or perhaps her inner strength has awakened to be strong for herself - but more and more, I see her energetically taking a little bit more time to take care of herself and her own needs. She is finally advocating for herself and in that, I know, God is well pleased.

She's STRONG!

She's PASSIONATE!

She's A REAL SACRIFICER!

She's CARING!

She LOVES, and she is THE BEST MOTHER in the whole wide world to me!

I conclude this very special honoring of my mother by sharing her favorite hymn:

Through all the changing scenes of life, in trouble and in joy,
The praises of my God shall still, my heart and tongue employ.

Of his deliverance I will boast, till all that are distressed,
From my example, comfort take and lay their griefs to rest.

O magnify the LORD with me, exalt his holy name;
When in distress to him I called, he to my rescue.

The hosts of God encamp around the dwellings of the just;
deliverance he affords to all who in his promise trust.

Co-author Dr. Vida-Lynn Asare's mother, Grace Adwoa Sekyere

From Dr. Karen's Desk

IN GRATEFUL CONCLUSION

MAMA, TAKE A BOW!

My aim for this project is to highlight the incredible strength, resilience, and amazingness that a Black mother is. It is to honor and lift the legacies of an often misunderstood group of people whose stories have not been told enough. No, she may not have been famous, written a book, gone to the moon, or been the head of state; but she surely gave life to those of us, who are now determined to tell her story. She is giving birth again through this token of honor. She is nurturing still through her legacy. She is being applauded for her selfless sacrifices. Her presence in this realm impacted, directed and, in some cases, re-directed generations with her one act – being her and being here. A mother behind a veil, in the shadows, a mother dishonored, ignored, and even despised now takes a bow as we revel in who she is or was.

Our goal for this compilation is to give and reconcile relationships of children of Black mothers, and impact generations – one story at a time. The writing process, prompts, activities, and methods used to pen these stories were designed in a way to capture stories that honorably reframe those narratives with which we once struggled. But now they intentionally appreciate and respect them as they have surely evolved as mature women, community leaders, businesswomen, entrepreneurs, wives, mothers, and grandmothers.

A WRITING BLUEPRINT FOR WRITING YOUR MOTHER'S STORY

Writing a memoir or narrative about a loved one can be rewarding and healing. Dr. Karen created a few self-reflective techniques with her authors such as WritetheBridgeWay, WriteDown2theRoots, Write2Heal, Write2Reveal, and TransformtheWriteWay to name a few. Below are a few of the Writing Activities you could use to begin the process if you are interested:

Gathering artifacts: Prepare by gathering pics, memories and quotes of your mother. Think of who you would want to interview and where would you find historical tidbits about her – education, childhood, degrees, career, hobbies, family tree, etc.

Interviews: Think of who you would want to interview and where would you find historical tidbits about your mother. Consider – education, childhood, degrees, career, hobbies, family tree, etc. Who will you interview? In your family, her places of employment, school records?

DR. KAREN'S WRITING PROMPTS:

What do you admire most about mom?

A short story that captures who she is/was?

Narrow down three words to describe your mom.

How has/did she change(d) over the years?

What would she want you to write about her in a book?

What do you think she would say?

If your mom could relive her life, what would she do differently?

What would she never change?

What specific outcome do you want to see from this book?

What will it cost you to NOT create this outcome?

What is the one thing you want to say to your Mother / about your Mother?

MATTERS OF THE HEART: QUESTIONS TO PONDER:

What about this AMAZING collaboration inspired you to want to write?

Describe the most important thing you want to learn, change, reframe or accomplish with writing about your mother?

Do you need to heal? Have you considered therapy, counseling, journaling, etc.?

WRITING ACTIVITIES AND RESOURCES TO INSPIRE YOUR BEST WRITING:

Think about creating an overarching guiding question or statement to guide your writing.

Begin adding story intro/elements into Writing Guide Template created by Dr. Karen (email Bridgewayteam444@gmail.com)

Use the questions to help with the reframing

Set a timer and write for seven, uninterrupted minutes about your mother.

Write a love letter to or from your mother

Using Psalm 139 as framework, write a Love Letter from the Father to yourself. Replace with your name in each place "me" is recorded, and feel the Father's love.

Use, the "Power in the Voice" recordings

Purchase a Writing Guide Template from #TheWriteRemedyCoach

Blessings & Bridges,
Dr. Karen L. Maxfield-Lunkin

MEET THE FABULOUS CO-AUTHORS

ANGELA TAITT

With over 20 years of counseling experience, and in active pursuit of her master's in social work for fall of 2022, Angela Taitt has prided herself on working in diverse mental health environments. Passionate about empowering women through her new initiative, P.I.N.K. Boss Lady LLC, Angela believes that any woman through belief can achieve the best version of herself. Active in ministry for over 20 years, Angela is a licensed Missionary Evangelist for the Church of God In Christ. Residing in Temple, TX with her newlywed husband, she is a mother of four, grandmother of three, and is the eldest of two children. In her downtime Angela enjoys continuing to work on her self-love journey and attend family events. You can keep in touch with Angela at pinkbossladycoach@gmail.com or www.pinkbosslady.com.

FELECIA KAMBERLY ROSE

Hailing from Itta Bena, Mississippi and currently residing in the Dallas suburb of Garland, Texas Felecia Kamberly Rose Phillips is a poet as well as a model, minister, and mother of one adult son, Christian Alexander Philips. Known for her witty writing, Felecia strives to be a conduit of change in ministry as well as in the marketplace. You can follow her on all things social media by searching for her name on Facebook, Instagram, and LinkedIn as well as a stage near you!

KESHIA SHONETTE SANDERS

South Carolina State University graduate Keshia Shonette Sanders currently resides in Austin, Texas. The Marion, South Carolina native currently holds a Bachelor of Science degree in Business Administration/Management and is an active member of the Alpha Kappa Alpha Sorority, Incorporated. Ms. Sanders is an Emergency Management Specialist for the Department of Homeland Security. Also an entrepreneur, she is the founder and President of KL3 Documents and Solutions, LLC.

Serving over two decades as a federal contractor in the DC Metro Area in Maryland, with the Department of Health and Human Services and the Department of Commerce, Keshia has gained expertise in records, graphic design, and project management. As a licensed minister and 2nd Vice President of SURE Ministries, Inc, Dallas, TX, she served in the ministry of Community and Women's Outreach. Keshia is the proud godmother of Brian, Erin, and Karleigh. To date, Keshia's favorite scripture is Philippians 4:13.

LONNETTA M. ALBRIGHT

Lonnetta Albright, author, radio personality, change agent, and facilitator is one of the most dynamic and transformative speakers, facilitators and coaches working nationally and internationally (Africa, the Caribbean, and South America) adding value to and changing the lives of thousands. She is particularly focused on developing those she fondly calls the"Next Generation." As President/Owner of Forward Movement Inc., she offers Executive and Life Coaching; Personal and Professional growth; Organizational and Leadership development; Speaking, Consulting and Facilitation.

A certified personal and executive coach, she is an Executive Director with the John Maxwell Team. Her expertise lies not only in connecting with clients and audiences; but also, her ability to take complex ideas and concepts, breaking them down into practical and thought-provoking blocks and presenting that same information in an exciting, learnable, and inspirational way. Her approaches and strategies are not just about personal and professional development – she helps her clients get results! Her popular "Heart-Mind Time (HMT)" program has impacted countless lives!

REVEREND MATILDA ADAMS

Ordained Minister, Matilda Adams is a Board-Certified Executive Nurse by profession and has accepted her Kingdom assignment to strengthen the body of Christ through the preaching and teaching of the word of God and intercession. Her vision is to see the body of Christ grow in the power and manifestation of the Holy Spirit. Living the mantra of the Apostle Paul – that she may be all things to all men that she may win some (1 Corinthians 9:22). President and CEO of Maybridge Healthcare Services, wife and mother of four, Reverend Adams is known for her heart and compassion as well as her love and commitment for all things God, and is known to be a prisoner of HOPE!

Dr. L. Michelle McCormick

Wife, mother, grandmother, author, life coach, and pastor, Dr. Michelle McCormick makes it known by her daily walk, that Jesus is the lover of her soul. It is her relationship with Christ which has been the healing balm in her life. Wife of Robert McCormick, mother of five children with two bonus sons; and grandmother of twenty, Dr. McCormick has her doctorate degree in Christian Theology.

Author of "Behind the Mask", as well as the founder and CEO of Victim to Victory Coaching, LLC, a company dedicated to transitioning people from a victim mindset to a victorious one, Dr. McCormick had a rough start to life, thus she lives her life according to Romans 8:28, "And we know that all things work together for good to those who love God, to those who are the called according to His purpose." You can keep up with all things Dr. Michelle McCormick at www.victimtovictorycoach.com.

RHONDA ETHERIDGE

Temple, Texas native Rhonda Etheridge was born to Kate and Sullivan Stephen. Wife of 34 years to Bruce Etheridge and mother of three children, two boys and one girl, Rhonda has been an educator for most of her life. Working and volunteering her time to both students and teachers, Rhonda has helped countless people who need mentorship and coaching in their roughest moments. A principal for 15 years, Rhonda has always had a desire to help others grow in their strengthens and seeing them become great individuals. She has always been that voice of encouragement not only for her children as they are high achievers themselves in Political Science, Accounting, and one on track to graduate in Computer Science. Rhonda continues to be a voice to the voiceless as she's had the opportunity to study at the international level the values and impacts of educational systems and sat on several academic committees. Rhonda continuously demonstrates the capability to develop and create programs and successfully promote both student and teacher alike. You can stay in touch with Rhonda by email at RhondaEtheridge.Re@gmail.com

STANLEY SENIOR

Retired marketing professional Stanley Senior is the third and youngest child born to Jewell Senior. Graduating from Santa Monica High School lettering in basketball and track, Stanley went on to serve in the United States Air Force prior to returning to school and obtaining his associates and bachelor's degree in marketing. Working in marketing for over a decade, Stanley then decided to open his own business as a personal trainer and later as a realtor and earned million-dollar status on one occasion. Stanley then began working in the travel and transportation industry for five years driving limousines and party vehicles, finalizing his career by working for Google and retiring in 2018 becoming a world traveler. Stanley firmly believes he has captured the essence of his mother in every way. You can keep up with Stanley and his photography at stanmanworld.com or on Facebook at Stanley.senior.3

TRINA WILKINS

Hackensack, New Jersey native Trina Wilkins currently resides in Roanoke, Virgina. A current graduate of Spring Arbor University with a Bachelor of Arts Degree in Family Life Education and a Master of Arts Degree in Human Service with a Marriage and Family Counseling Focus in 2015, Trina has worked in the social work arena for over a decade. Currently a Care Coordinator for United Healthcare, Trina enjoys helping others improve their lifestyles. Trina prides herself on taking time to explore the arts, reading, traveling, and being creative and crafty. You can connect with Trina on Instagram at Tretre74 or on LinkedIn by searching for Trina Wilkins.

Dr. Vida-Lynn Asare

Dr. Vida-Lynn Asare is a Bible teacher and a Nurse Practitioner who has touched many lives with her love of the Lord, compassion, and exemplary personality. She is married to Rev. Charles Asare and their marriage is blessed with three wonderful children: Steve, Lady Charlene, and Vida-Michelle.

Raised by a prayerful grandmother and a God-fearing mother who instilled Godly values into Dr. Vida and her nine siblings, is a testament to this parenting style and the grace of God that all her siblings and more than twenty nieces. Each has allowed God to use them in various ministries for the expansion of His Kingdom. She accepted Jesus Christ as her Lord and personal savior at the age of 13 and has never looked back. Her most celebrated awards are her service to the Lord, her family, and empowering other women.

Vida-Lynn holds a strong belief about sharing the Gospel of Christ. She is also passionate about nurturing women to live out the fullest potential that God gave them. The Lord has led her to organize the Revealing Grace prayer ministry to build and support women in their prayer lives.

She is an alumnus of Stony Brook, Rutgers, and Chatham

universities. She holds a doctorate in nursing practice and also practices as an Adult Nurse Practitioner in Internal Medicine.

Her life's journey and faith are strengthened by Isaiah 40: 31 "But those who wait on the Lord shall renew their strength; they shall mount up with wings like eagles, they shall run and not be weary they shall walk and not faint.

Visionary Author and Writing Coach, Dr. Karen Maxfield-Lunkin

is a best-selling, award winning, literary coach and visionary author, an educational entrepreneur with more than 30 years of experience as a parent, teacher, pastor, mentor, school principal, professor, parent-coach and educational advocate. Described as a thought leader and innovator, Dr. Karen's mission is to "guide people through writing to *un*cover - to *dis*cover and finally *re*cover their God-given gifts and talents buried within to be about their Kingdom Business."

Dr. Karen enjoys inspiring aspiring authors to write and publish. A guest lecturer and adjunct university professor, and involved in numerous community initiatives, including chairwoman of the board of directors for an African Diaspora group in Austin, Texas, Dr. Karen finds inspiration to write in all things!

Known on social media as the #WriteRemedyCoach, Dr. Karen loves coaching authors to discovery, transformation and healing.

An ordained minister, Dr. Karen is also the founder of Bridge

Kingdom Ministries, a nonprofit organization with the mission to actively explore and engage in opportunities for edu-preneurial connection between teachers and schools in Ghana and teachers of children in impoverished neighborhoods in the US; Inspire teachers and students to recognize that the Kingdom of God is already within and all we need is already in our hands.

Bridging all in the African Diaspora to face and heal from the past traumas our ancestral past with the "twist" of approaching the past with forgiveness, and creative determination to reframe present conditions through the lens of God's Word.

Residing in Austin, Texas with Michael, her husband of thirty-three years, they have three grown children, and two rescue dogs.

Made in the USA
Middletown, DE
20 October 2022

13128687R00073